Come Together

Come Together:
the years of gay liberation (1970–73)

edited and introduced by

Aubrey Walter

VERSO
London • New York

This edition published by Verso 2018
First published in Great Britain by Gay Men's Press 1980
Selection and Introduction © Aubrey Walter 1980, 2018

1 3 5 7 9 10 8 6 4 2

Verso
UK: 6 Meard Street, London W1F 0EG
US: 20 Jay Street, Suite 1010, Brooklyn, NY 11201
versobooks.com

Verso is the imprint of New Left Books

ISBN-13: 978-1-78873-237-6
ISBN-13: 978-1-78873-238-3 (UK EBK)
ISBN-13: 978-1-78873-239-0 (US EBK)

British Library Cataloguing in Publication Data
A catalogue record for this book is available from the British Library

Library of Congress Cataloging-in-Publication Data
A catalog record for this book is available
from the Library of Congress

Printed and bound by CPI Group (UK) Ltd, Croydon, CR0 4YY

Introduction

It is now common knowledge that the gay liberation movement started in New York in June 1969, when the queens in the Stonewall bar fought back police repression, and for the first time in history gay people began to stand up on a massive scale. The movement spread like a forest fire, first across the United States, then soon catching on in the rest of the Western world. In this intense struggle for the social recognition of homosexuality, a certain gay consciousness was formed.

The essence of this new consciousness was gay pride. Gay pride meant that the homosexual individual no longer accepted the heterosexist society's definition of him/herself as criminal, pathetic or sick. It meant that at long last the lesbian and gay man could raise their heads with the deep inner conviction that homosexuality was part and parcel of the human package, seeing the roles imposed on women and men by the present sexist society as perverse, rather than the homosexuals who reject them. The growth of gay pride could only be a collective process. Only if gay people gained strength from solidarity and organisation could they advance their liberation and spread the new message. And in this way countless numbers of lesbians and gay men gained the necessary courage and strength to come out of their double-life hellholes and closets and confront the straight world around them.

As the gay liberation struggle developed, the positive aspects of homosexuality became ever more clear. Unlike heterosexuality, homosexuality was already completely free from any connection with biological procreation. In the context of a sexist society, moreover, our sexuality was not based on the subjugation of one sex by another. Gay relationships were far less structured by male domination and the gender system, while in straight relationships the temptation to fall back into the gender pattern is overwhelmingly strong, no matter how intensely individuals try and fight against it.

The London Gay Liberation Front *Manifesto* of 1971 shows the high point reached by the new gay consciousness, a level which the gay movement of today, unfortunately, often fails to match:

> Gay shows the way. In some ways we are *already* more advanced than straight people. We are already outside the family and we have already, in part at least, rejected the 'masculine' or 'feminine' roles society has designed for us. In a society dominated by the sexist culture it is very difficult, if not impossible, for heterosexual men and women to escape their rigid gender-role structuring and the roles of oppressor and oppressed. But gay men don't need to oppress women in order to fulfil their own psycho-sexual needs, and gay women don't have to relate sexually to the male oppressor, so that at this moment in time, the freest and most equal relationships are most likely to be between homosexuals.*

Starting in the USA, the new gay movement learnt from the struggles of many other oppressed sectors in Western society. It learnt from the struggles of the women's movement, from the black movement, and from the movement against the imperialist war in Indochina. It was comparatively simple for people in the gay movement to make connections between the oppression they met from the forces of law and order, and that dealt out to other sectors. So, even though the gay movement always insisted on being fully autonomous, it could easily see itself as part of the wider struggle for full human rights and liberation.

In practical reality, however, the connection with other movements was not so easy. Many sectors of the radical movement opposed gay liberation, indeed most of the traditional left organisations initially saw homosexuals as mere 'decadent excrescences' on the body politic. Large sections of the women's movement were also sceptical and antagonistic at first, because at the turn of the 1970s lesbianism was only just becoming an issue in the movement and there was no adequate theory of sexism and gender. But by its tenacity, its militant activity, and by showing the courage of its convictions, gay liberation gradually began to whittle away opposition from the rest of the radical movement, even if its full significance is still very far from generally understood.

---

*   1979 edition, pp. 8-9. This is billed as a 'revised' edition of the original 1971 *Manifesto*. In fact, it is a straightforward reprint, apart from the crucial section 'Aims'. See below, p. 21.

The Birth of London GLF

During the first year of GLF in the United States, most gay men and lesbians in Britain were unaware of what was happening on the other side of the Atlantic. There were very occasional reports in the press, such as in spring 1970 when gay liberationists disrupted a psychiatric conference in San Francisco. About this gay man Konstantin Berlandt running round in a red lamé dress and long wig, as one of a group of 'gay guerillas' protesting the treatment and definitions of homosexuality by the US psychiatric establishment. It was intriguing for me to read these reports, but very hard to fit them into my ideas about politics, especially politics in England. When I visited North America in summer 1970, one of my main objects was to find out about the new gay movement. I stayed with GLF groups in one city after another, and it really changed the way that I looked at my own homosexuality, and the

question of gender in general. It was there that I got to know Bob
Mellors, who was hanging out with New York GLF. We met at
the 'Revolutionary Peoples' Constitutional Convention' in
Philadelphia, called by the Black Panther Party. Not only did gay
liberationists go to Philadelphia to show solidarity with the black
movement, but it was here that Huey Newton, as leader of the
Panthers, first gave clear support to the gay cause, saying that
homosexuals were maybe the most oppressed people in American
society, and could well be the most revolutionary.*

Christopher Street demo, New York (summer 1970)

---

*   See 'A Letter from Huey' in Len Richmond and Gary Noguera (eds), *The
     Gay Liberation Book*, San Francisco, 1973, pp. 142-45.

Bob Mellors and I decided that when we got back to London we would call a meeting to organise a GLF there. During that summer, however, the first sparks of the new gay consciousness were already beginning to fly in Britain. A gay freak, Dave Burke, wrote to the California newspaper *Gay Sunshine* about how bad the London gay scene was for 'heads' like himself, and a small group demonstrated in September against the editors of the London University newspaper *Sennet*, for their anti-gay sentiments. The time was clearly ripe for GLF to take off in Britain, too.

The first meeting of London GLF took place on 13th October 1970, in a basement classroom at the London School of Economics, where Bob was a student. Nineteen people came to that first meeting, one woman, the rest gay men, and Bob and I spoke about GLF in the States and our experiences there. I think we were still rather full of American rhetoric and gay liberation jargon which many of those present didn't really understand, slogans such as 'We gotta get out of the ghetto', and 'Out of the closets and into the streets'. The meeting, though small, was extremely intense. After much discussion we agreed to publicise the next meeting much more, and to spread the news. Several people who came to that first meeting were to remain active in London GLF throughout its life.

During its first few weeks, GLF was sort of blind, in that even though it had a real sense of purpose, it had no defined principles on which to organise, or demands for which to struggle. The more political people felt a sense of frustration along with the general exhilaration, and realised that some clearer definition of our goals was needed. First a list of basic Demands was drawn up and put onto a leaflet, which we distributed in the gay areas of West London. The response was overwhelming. Hundreds of new people flocked to the meetings to see what this new movement was all about. This gave the early GLF activists an enormous fillip, as it showed that there was indeed a large reservoir of energy, just waiting to engage in our struggle. In mid-November the Demands were modified and improved, and in this form they were printed in the first issue of *Come Together* and reproduced countless times from then on.

The Principles were drafted by David Fernbach and myself, and presented to the general meeting in early December, where they were overwhelmingly adopted. One extra paragraph, however, dealing with the threat of fascism, was rejected after it divided the meeting. The Demands and Principles together gave

GLF a more coherent identity and direction, as it grew into a real mass movement. But even though GLF now defined itself as 'part of the wider movement aiming to abolish all forms of social oppression', the Principles still didn't really explain our oppression in terms of the basic structures of society. The Principles pointed to 'the structure of the family', but we still didn't have any real theory of gender, and fell back on explaining homophobia as a 'prejudice'. In other words, we hadn't yet developed our own gay critique of the present society, in which institutionalised hetero-sexuality goes hand in hand with male supremacy. This would only come later, with the publication of the GLF *Manifesto* in October 1971.

With all the new people coming in, we had to move to a larger room, and within a few weeks to LSE's New Theatre, to accom-modate a couple of hundred people. The meetings in the New Theatre were really exciting, and it was here that the spirit of GLF began to take shape, even though a lecture theatre is not all that conducive to a democratic type of meeting.

On November 27th, GLF held its first public demonstration. By this time, what with all the energy that had been generated, people were itching to make some sort of militant stand against oppression. That Friday evening we assembled by Highbury and Islington station, and marched arm-in-arm to Highbury Fields, where a prominent Young Liberal had been arrested by the police and accused of 'indecency'. I remember this as a very exhilarating moment for homosexuals in Britain, to actually be banded together in public for the first time, holding hands and shouting our 'Give us a G' slogan. Burning torches were distri-buted, and we kissed warmly and perhaps a little dramatically for the press. We all felt so tremendously high. The lesbians in GLF also organised a very successful leafleting of the Gateways Club, Britain's best-known lesbian meeting-place. But all the time, GLF people were making their presence felt by coming out publicly. Wherever we went, travelling on bus or tube, or simply walking down the streets, we would flaunt our homosexuality, challenging straight people to put us down, so to speak, precisely so that we could fight back.

Those gay men and lesbians who had constructed a comfortable niche for themselves in the conventional 'straight gay' closet, soon began to get very disturbed by all these out, militant gay liberationists. They really hated GLF for rocking their boat. It was already clear to us at the time, however, that we were having a very real effect on the gay community, and were even pushing the uptight traditional gay organisations towards a more militant stand — we were challenging them to come out.

How representative were the people who came into GLF of the gay community at large? In some ways they were very typical, in other ways rather less so. It was immediately obvious at any GLF function that the great majority were under 30 years old. There were also significantly high numbers of artists and intellectuals, self-employed people and drop-outs, all of whom had less to lose by joining an aggressively blatant gay movement. There were perhaps five times more men than women. But the majority of GLF supporters were fairly typical of young gay men and lesbians in the metropolitan area. They mainly worked in shops and offices, or in minor professional jobs, or else they were still studying. Very few were factory workers, but very few, too, had any significant class privilege.

Very early on we recognised that if we were to attract people from the gay community we had to create an alternative social scene to the existing gay pubs and clubs. We held our first GLF disco at LSE on December 4th, 1970, and our first GLF Peoples' Dance on December 22nd at Kensington Town Hall. Publicly advertised gay dances such as this were as much a political event as a social one. The struggle for the right to book public facilities such as town halls for gay purposes was a very important strand in expanding the social space for gay people. Our general meetings, conversely, were always exciting social occasions as well as political. When the actual meeting was over, people would mill around talking for ages, and then spill over into the nearest pub to continue their socialising and heated discusssions.

Media Workshop and Come Together

After only a few general meetings, however, we began to realise that these large meetings were all very well for making us feel good and for arousing our massed enthusiasm, but were hopeless for getting anything very practical done. The idea spread of setting up more specialised 'functional' groups. Media Workshop, which was to start *Come Together*, was the first of these, and before Christmas there was also a Psychiatry Study Group to attack the myths put out by bourgeois psychiatry, a Street Theatre Group, a Demonstrations Group, a Women's Group, an Education Group and a Schools Group. Consciousness-raising groups, or awareness groups as we called them, were also beginning to form. It was stressed time and again that the real work of GLF took place in these functional groups.

We soon became aware of how difficult it was going to be to spread the gay liberation message around the country, even around London. It was easy enough to reach the minority of gays in the ghetto of Earl's Court. But the vast majority of gay men and lesbians hardly ever went to gay pubs, clubs or discos. And however inadequate the facilities for gays in London, in the rest of the country the situation was very much worse. Our target had to be the silent majority stuck in their lonely closets, too isolated, afraid and intimidated to come out. But we were still small and weak ourselves. GLF had no funds or even an office until well into 1971, and the mass media were more or less closed to gays — aside from the isolated radio interview, or a television programme with all the homosexual participants in silhouette.

Yet despite the way that the cards were stacked against us, the gay liberation message did get through. The gay grapevine is bigger than many people think. During 1971, gay liberation groups spontaneously organised themselves in Birmingham, Manchester, Bristol, Cardiff, Edinburgh, Leeds and elsewhere. People would get to hear about GLF from friends who had been in London, or people who perhaps were already involved in CHE (then still the 'Committee' for Homosexual Equality) would want something more open and militant. Somehow or other they would contact each other and form a GLF group. These would often start up around the universities, because rooms were more readily available for meetings, etc.

One of the reasons for setting up Media Workshop was to develop our own channels to push the ideas of gay liberation. Media Workshop met regularly from November 1970 to the end of 1971, and produced the first ten issues of *Come Together*, apart from number 7, a women's issue. The first couple of issues were simple, duplicated broadsheets given out free at GLF meetings and to the gay community. The name *Come Together* was chosen for its triple entendre: the communal or collectivist aspiration, the sexual reference, and the John Lennon song of the time. It was to last for 16 issues altogether, finally fading away in mid-1973. In its pages it reflected the turbulent growth, history and development of the gay liberation movement, and almost every idea and practice that gained currency found expression in the paper.

Putting out *Come Together* was a great collectivist experience, in that everyone who attended Media Workshop meetings had an equal say in what went in. Articles coming in to Media Workshop would be thoroughly read and discussed collectively by the group, before being typed out, pasted up, etc. Only very rarely did Media Workshop feel it had to reject material, and this was usually on a well thought-out basis, because of an article's overt sexism or something similar. We started out feeling that we had to include everything we got in, and even when this proved impractical, we continued to be as little restrictive as possible.

It was also a great activity to go around selling the paper, especially in Earl's Court, where you could get into fairly heated discussions in the gay pubs. Many of the articles in *Come Together* created quite a stir even at the general meetings of GLF, where they would be heavily praised or criticised. Some of the early radical feminist ideas that came to England from the United States were in articles we reprinted from the New York paper *Come Out*, by people such as Martha Shelley and Steve Dansky.*

Organisation

GLF meetings were indeed very democratic. Everyone who had something to say had a chance to speak. And people who had remained silent all their lives about their oppression, at last had a forum where they could speak up and where others like them would listen sympathetically to what they had to say. One of the strongest elements in the GLF ideology, in fact, was a basic libertarianism that was very much against the star system, elitism, bureaucracy, and strong leadership structures. People would say that hierarchical organisation was part of the straight (i.e. hetero-sexist) system that had oppressed us for so long, and that we should not emulate our enemy but attempt to create our own type of structure, one that was basically freer, more open and democratic — 'After all, who needs leaders? We're not sheep but free, beautiful, gay human beings.'

Our general meetings were held every Wednesday, and they would be packed with curious and excited homosexuals. But although the ideology said 'no leaders', we still had to have something to make sure that the meetings worked, and that there was some sort of continuity from one week to the next. So, very early on a steering committee was elected, with a circulating chairperson and recallable at any time, to make sure that decisions agreed at the general meetings were actually carried out, and to draw up the agenda for the next meeting.

If the movement was to have any real shape and direction,

---

* I haven't reprinted either of the two Martha Shelley articles here, as they're available in other anthologies.

then some type of centre was certainly necessary. But many of the most active people were themselves very worried by the emergence of any leading committee. They could see the danger that this would ossify and become merely bureaucratic, like so many other organisations. One way to avoid this dilemma was sought through the think-in, an unstructured conference that was to become the main forum in which policy and direction was determined and argued out. The first think-in was held at LSE in January 1971, and this helped to solidarise the GLF core against the machinations of Anthony Grey of the Albany Trust, who had played a leading role in pushing through the Sexual Offences Act of 1967. He was attempting to capture the energy of GLF for the cause of respectable pressure-group politics, but was roundly defeated by our concerted efforts. Throughout its short history, GLF had a series of think-ins, and all major decisions that affected the movement's organisational development were taken in this way.

The think-ins were organised in as democratic a manner as possible. The practice of breaking down into small discussion groups, which was applied at the think-ins, and for a time also in the all-London general meetings, was designed to counter the domination of GLF by those people whose university education or simply bigger egos set them at an unfair advantage in debates over policy and tactics. This system of workshops enabled the great majority of people who attended a big meeting to contribute to the discussions and outcome. Think-ins were first held in London, but as GLF spread across the country there were later national think-ins in Leeds, Birmingham and Lancaster. The think-in was also an arena where new ideas were floated and spread.

Most people found the early think-ins very exciting affairs indeed. They were not simply talking-shops, but week-end venues where we felt very much that we were on gay territory, where the participants shared quite a bit of common ground, and where we could argue as open gays about the problems of *our* movement, without having to fight against uptight and neurotic heterosexuals who saw homosexuality as a problem. There were certainly many violent clashes and disagreements, but these were disagreements among equals; we were able to avoid the syndrome of having panels of 'experts' and 'authorities' presiding over us and handing down their 'wisdom'.

By early 1971, London GLF badly felt the need for an office and a telephone line from which information could be collated and spread about, particularly for new people wanting to find out about and come into the gay movement. A small office was found in the basement of *Peace News* in Caledonian Road. An office collective was formed so that this could be staffed on a rota basis. Small meetings were also held there.

Because the office collective now took on the everyday running of things, the original steering committee became more and more redundant. There were also problems with steering committee members making public statements on behalf of GLF which went beyond their authority, and the general meetings accordingly became somewhat chaotic. The steering committee simply could not handle the meetings and the criticism it was getting, and there came a time when it would resign each week. A new proposal was then adopted by the general meeting, in April 1971, for a coordinating committee of a more ongoing nature. This was made up of representatives from the various functional groups. It met at the GLF office and drew up the agenda, etc. for the general meeting, as the steering committee had originally been mandated to do. But even though the new coordinating committee worked quite well, there was to remain a constant tension between the needs of central coordination and the democratic aspirations of the base, which later came to focus in hostility to the office collective.

During the first two months of 1971 we were still meeting at LSE, though we had also met for a few weeks at the Arts Lab over the Christmas period. Eventually the LSE authorities objected to these large meetings on their premises, and threw us out. We then moved on to Middle Earth, a rambling basement disco in King Street, Covent Garden. The new environment gave these meetings added colour, but also made them a bit of a spectacle. People would come from all over the place, and it became part of the trendy London scene to pay a visit and show one's face at the GLF meeting. We would mill around in the gloomy depths, small meetings would be taking place in different corners, as well as the main general meeting. Eventually we had to leave Middle Earth too, and since many GLF activists were living in the Notting Hill area, some people managed to book the All Saints church hall in Powis Square. We moved there in July, and by this time London GLF was at the peak of its activity, with weekly meetings of 500 and more.

Awareness Groups

We first started to form awareness groups in December 1970. This was seen as an essential part of gay liberation activity, and one that was increasingly necessary for activists going through quite fast and fundamental changes to the whole fabric of their lives. After all, gay liberation was not something we did only on Wednesdays at the general meetings, it was rather a totally lived-through experience.

We took over the concept of consciousness-raising from the United States. Consciousness-raising groups were in fact common place in the States among people involved in the radical movement of the late 1960s. The idea really came from the experiences of the Chinese revolution, as explained in the widely read book *Fanshen* by William Hinton, an account of revolution in a Chinese village. This describes how the poor and landless peasants who had been oppressed for millenia by the ruthless landlord and bureaucratic class were encouraged by the Communist Party to talk about their lives until everyone began to deeply understand how their particular individual fates were all linked up, that their sufferings were in no way their own fault, but that they were all victims of a particular social system. Likewise in gay consciousness-raising, from each individual talking about his or her individual experience of oppression, growing up, coming out, etc., a general pattern could be discerned, and so a cognitive leap would take place in the minds of the group. They would then come to see the oppression of gay people as part of the general gender system of our society, with common features despite individual idiosyncracies. These awareness groups were particularly important given how self-oppression plays such an insidious part in the oppression of gay people. We have all adopted and internalised so much of the straight society's values.

That was the theory, though not all of our awareness groups actually worked like that. They were all very different, and meant different things to different people. But they all did provide an essential support group for us in undergoing basic changes, a place where we could voice our deeper feelings about things, where we could share our experiences. For example, a group might decide to focus on a different individual member each week. So everyone in turn would go through their life and upbringing. There was to be no putting on of images, you had to be honest, and if you found this difficult, then the other members would try to help you overcome your fear of facing up to who you really were. It could be very painful, especially for those who had bottled up their feelings inside themselves nearly all their lives. And of course people grew very close to each other. Some of the emotions let loose could be very, very heavy; there were often interpersonal battles in these awareness groups, and some people even became enemies. It was an unwritten rule that couples should always be in separate groups, otherwise they would start playing their couple games and other people would be at a disadvantage.

When a group had been through all the hang-ups and histories, it might then go on to other things, such as body exploration, dressing up in drag, group sex, or theoretical discussions. Many awareness groups broke up and split apart, others went on for a couple of years and their members became life-long friends. Usually your awareness group became the most important event of the week, not to be missed at any cost. By simply missing out on one meeting, you felt as if you were not quite part of things any more, and it would take a lot of reassuring from the others to bring you back. Everything moved so fast; people would undergo fundamental change almost overnight. A rather closety, straight-ish, butch, hirsute man would emerge as a screaming, freaky queen; a shy, self-conscious person might become confident and articulate.

It became the policy in GLF to try and help new people coming in to join up with an awareness group. And eventually the GLF office put out a leaflet on awareness groups and the experience of consciousness-raising, and regularly informed people of new groups being started.

Alternative Lifestyle

GLF was certainly in the business of attempting to create an alternative lifestyle for gay people. Our conception of politics was so very different from both the straight male left and the more respectable gay organisations. Right from the start we deliberately attempted to be different, to at least try and break down the barriers of hostility between individuals. Most of us tried to show outward signs of love to each other. It became more or less obligatory for people to kiss each other on greeting or leaving, at meetings, in the street or wherever. Of course, this sometimes became a convention with little meaning, but it did give GLF a more together external image, more solidarised and collective, less aggressive and male, an image that was consciously seen as alternative. In many ways this followed on from the innovations of the women's movement, though GLF had its own quite distinct style; the similarity perhaps reflected a basic libertarianism in both movements. We would consciously at first, unconsciously later, touch, hold hands and hug, to show that we all cared for each other. I personally had never before known this kind of warm behaviour and sense of solidarity in any of my political involvements, except briefly perhaps during the violent clashes with the police in the demonstrations against US imperialism in Grosvenor Square of 1967-68. In fact the GLF style became catching, and many straight male politicos and freaks were forced to behave in a similar way to show that they were not uptight. Even today, gay activists continue this practice in their public behaviour.

Many of the men in GLF were seriously into analysing the images we were attempting to project, in particular the power of the butch image over our psyches. We were searching for something that was basically gender-free. This was to prove incredibly difficult, given that our core models were our heterosexual parents, so that even though we were calling for people to stop playing the roles offered by the 'straight gay' scene (which were simply reflections of the heterosexist world) and to be themselves, the question that kept arising was, 'Well, who are we anyway?' We had ourselves been conditioned by the gender system. The way round this dilemma was to upgrade the identification we had with our mothers, and so to push the more feminine qualities in our psyches and hence in our outward images and social behaviour.

People began to question the ways they lived out their lives, in isolated little boxes trying to ape their respectable straight counterparts. The idea of deliberately trying to construct an alternative lifestyle came of course from the straight counterculture, where people had already been involved for many years in alternative ways of living, such as urban collectives based on a shared work project, rural communes, etc., and to this extent what people in GLF were doing was nothing particularly new. In fact GLF was acting as a vehicle for many of the ideas and practices of the counterculture, and bringing them into the gay community for the first time. But there was a qualitative change in the concepts and practices of communal living once lesbians and gay men began to experiment with them. For the first time, people began to live communally on the basis of a shared sexuality. The straight hetero-communes, though having many progressive ideas about the way people should live, in terms of work sharing, property sharing, emotion sharing, etc., could be amazingly backward when it came down to sex roles and gender differentiation, and this is true to a large extent even today. Many communes, especially rural ones, were really into women being the playthings of men, the bearers and basic rearers of children and the ones who did most of the domestic work. The men would rationalise this backward approach with reference to 'mother nature' and the 'natural' order of things.*

When the ideas and personalities of the women's and gay movements entered the arena, people had to begin to think about real communalism based on the full equality of all human beings present. This meant that straight men had to give up their privileges based on the subjugation of women, to make the effort to open up to each other and not always lean on women for their emotional support. It meant that the socialisation of children should become the shared responsibility of everyone. A basic ethic of communal living was freedom to do whatever you wished as long as you didn't transgress anyone else's freedom. The rigid gender division so deeply rooted in the psyche of heterosexuals worked against this profound principle. Many of the gay communes that emerged during the period of GLF were committed to the libertarian ideal and were consciously against the gender conditioning pushed out by the nuclear family. As the GLF *Manifesto* pointed out:

> We intend to work for the replacement of the family unit with its rigid gender-role pattern by new organic units such as the commune, where the development of children becomes the shared responsibility of a larger group of people who live together. Children must be liberated from the present condition of having their role in life determined by biological accidents; the commune will ultimately provide a variety of gender-free models.**

---

* I attacked the sexism of the counterculture in an article written with David Fernbach, 'Wham, Bamn, Thank You Ma'am!' published in *7 Days*, 2nd-8th February 1972. A representative sample of what we were on about is quoted from this article by Jeffrey Weeks in *Coming Out*, p. 187.

** Original edition, p. 15. In the 1979 'revised' edition, all references to the replacement of the family by communes have been deleted! In the original *Manifesto*, we went on to say: 'We intend to start working out our contribution to these new models now, by creating an alternative gay culture free from sexism, and by setting up gay communes. When our communes are firmly established, we plan to let children grow up in them'. Unfortunately, the 'Gay Liberation Information Service' who reprinted the *Manifesto* seem to think this passage is too radical for the 1980s and might have a harmful effect on innocent young minds!

The actual problems of living together in a total way were really enormous, and many communes broke up very soon after formation. Others stuck it out and beautiful things emerged. People were aware that sexist ways of relating were not simply common to straight people, but were also deeply rooted amongst gay men and lesbians. They knew that they had to attempt to relate to each other not in terms of false ideas about good looks, etc., but in terms of accepting each other's basic humanity.

Communes in GLF were not just based on a shared sexuality, but also on ideological beliefs and commitments. Many gays who got into the politics of radical drag, for example, found it helped if they shared their lives together. In this way they were able to support each other in their courageous activities, particularly when they were constantly being reviled and put down by butch gay men and others who disagreed with them. In the community of gay men, queens have always occupied the lowest rung. It was the fem gays who got the worst deal, the ones who could not help but always be out. They are still despised and reviled even today by all those who say: 'They let us down, those queens, lisping and flapping their wrists like handkerchiefs'. In GLF the fem gay men had their revenge. After all it was they who had first fought back the repression, which they had experienced most. They still had a real struggle to make their voices heard. They had always been put down and made to feel inferior for their effeminacy. But the GLF message was, 'What's wrong with being effeminate, whatever that means?' After all, it was the butch, macho image that was doing all the harm.

So many gay men and even lesbians were ashamed of the out fem gays because they thought they only confirmed straight society's worst prejudices. Our answer was always: 'So what! Who wants to ape the images from the oppressive straight culture of what a man should be like?' In GLF people began to be really proud of being different from the so-called 'norm', and in 'being what gay is'. But where is this attitude today, how many times are fem gays still insulted and put down for being expressive with their hands, wrists and bodies, and for speaking in softer voices? The main images offered us by the gay ghetto are those of the would-be macho superbutches with their S & M undertones.

In GLF the butch image was seen to be really bad and oppressive for gay men. From a certain reading of radical feminism, many gays felt that in order to struggle against male privilege, they must do everything possible to show that they were prepared to give up this privilege in themselves. One way of doing so was to give up clothes which they termed as masculine, such as jeans and trousers, shirts and jackets, in favour of frocks, heels and make-up. In this way their rejection of male privilege was visibly apparent. One group into radical drag had a real confrontation when they set up a commune in Brixton right opposite a large comprehensive school. They would live in drag and go out in drag all the time. They soon attracted the attention of their neighbours, who on the whole didn't take too well to them, nor did the local schoolkids, who would lay siege to their house and throw bricks through their windows. But the radical drag people were an essential part of the GLF scene, and were always prominent in all GLF activities, on marches, Gay Days, etc. They were very much a part of what people thought of as 'Gay Lib'.

It wasn't just queens who got into the politics of drag. I can very well remember one person who had been straight, married and had a kid. He was a lecturer at a polytechnic. He got into the radical drag thing from having a guilt feeling about being male and having been straight, oppressing his wife and acting like a real 'man'. He would travel around wearing rather bizarre clothes, like a short sort of crimplene shift frock, rather run-down sling-backs, wild long thin hair, fairly conventional make-up and a handbag. Whenever he went on public transport he would be mocked and laughed at by people, and threatened and thrown off buses. So he developed this really aggressive manner of getting on tubes and buses, glaring around and threatening the other passengers first — he would also deliver his lectures in drag. Everyone thought he was really brave.

If this was an extreme example, serious commitment to GLF invariably did mean very major changes in personal life, and a far sharper confrontation with the straight world outside. As with most people involved in alternative lifestyles, the use of marijuana was fairly general, helping people to break down their internalisation of repressive social norms. When it came to questioning such fundamental things as gender identity, however, a more powerful solvent was required, and this was found above all in LSD. Acid was indeed a great help for many people in making and maintaining basic changes in their personalities and lifestyles, and for many GLF awareness groups, communes, etc., regular collective acid trips were central to their development. Acid was one of the secret dimensions of GLF. It was discussed in writing only in the most guarded of terms, though the 'schizophrenic' acid mentality shows through in several articles in *Come Together*. Yet LSD was an integral part of the GLF experience.

The ramifications of gay liberation in the counterculture, and in the search for alternative lifestyles opposed to the existence offered the masses by decaying capitalism and its consumerist death culture, are still being felt today. The struggle to live without gender patterning has in a way altered the whole terrain of the search for a new way of life.

Activities

Right from the start, GLF was a very action-oriented movement. Being a member of GLF — not that we ever had either formal membership or dues — meant that one had both the support and the courage to be actively gay in a public sense all or at least most of the time. The tone was set by our very first demonstration in Highbury Fields.

One of our main groups for organising zaps and demonstrations around many issues was Street Theatre, and they would travel the country to give examples of the sort of thing GLF was into. They actively supported many women's liberation struggles, beginning with the Miss World demonstration in 1970, when they held their own 'Miss Used' show outside the Albert Hall. One highlight of their activity was the back-street abortion they used to perform in our campaign against David Reuben's homophobic book *Everything You Always Wanted to Know About Sex*, complete with coat-hangers and raw liver, and plenty of convincing screams. We were all really impressed with the standard of their performance. It was the Street Theatre Group, too, who were behind Operation Rupert against the Festival of Light, described in *Come Together* 9 and 10, in fact a series of actions in which GLF gave extremely effective leadership to a coalition of forces who mobilised against the Festival.

Another of our functional groups, the Counter-Psychiatry Group, organised a demonstration in Harley Street, against bourgeois psychiatry and its oppression of gay people. The evening before the actual demonstration took place, several of us met at Regent's Park tube station with our shoulder- and handbags full of spray-paint cans, and covered the whole length of Harley Street with slogans. It certainly looked pretty the next day, with our beautiful red slogans painted over the respectable facade of this symbol of private medicine for the rich and oppression for the deviant.

GLF were often thrown out of gay pubs and clubs when we attempted to leaflet them or talk to the people there, the Gateways bust described in *Come Together* 4 being one early example.

When the general meetings moved to Notting Hill in summer 1971, the local police organised the publicans in the neighbourhood to ban GLF from using their facilities. Through a series of demos and sit-ins, we successfully upheld our right to use these pubs, and behave in the manner that was natural to us.

We participated in many broad left demos of the time, too, e.g. on issues which affected gay men and lesbians as workers. When a hundred or so of us went on the giant anti-Industrial Relations Bill demo in February 1971, we met with a characteristically mixed reception from other groups. Most of these viewed us with bemusement, if not outright hostility. We were shunted right to the back of the march, because other socialist groups and trade unions were ashamed to be seen with a group of 'perverts' on their ever so respectably militant demo against the Heath government. Gays were also vilified during demonstrations against the US imperialist war of aggression in Indochina. Many groups carrying their banners of Marx, Engels, Lenin, etc. would scream at us that we were the scum of the earth (victims of capitalism like prostitutes, so some of their theorists called us, degenerate elements who were against the 'socialist family'). Even in 1972 I can remember a demo when a GLF contingent was violently ejected by the IS (now the ever so right-on-to-gay-rights SWP). The first groups on the left who began to give the gay liberation movement any sort of support were the more libertarian and anarchist groups. All the others were into protecting their very 'proletarian' revolutionary image so as not to offend 'the working class'. It obviously didn't occur to them that most lesbians and gay men happen to be working class themselves.

During the summers of 1971 and 1972, GLF also organised some very beautiful Gay Days in parks throughout the London area. There were often two or even three of these each weekend. People would get together, sit around talking, laughing and smiling, holding each other, touching, playing games of various kinds. Straight people would often gather round and watch these crazy gays, and many would themselves join in and have a good time. As with our dances, the political struggle to expand our space went hand in hand with creating a very different social scene for gay people.

August 1971 saw our first carnival-type demo. This was really the first celebration of Gay Pride in Britain, and we marched from Marble Arch to Trafalgar Square, to hear our non-leaders give little speeches from the podium. Half of us were up there, too, so it was all very democratic.

*The GLF Manifesto
and the Backlash
Against It*

The GLF Principles had presented the struggle for gay liberation
as one of several parallel struggles of oppressed groups: they had
been strongly influenced by the American Black Panthers' theory
of 'intercommunalism'. By summer 1971, however, certain problems were arising that reflected contradictions between different
'communities', and which the Principles couldn't resolve. One
particular occasion was the trial of *OZ* magazine, a leading
underground paper of the time, on charges of 'obscenity'. The
Women's Group of GLF, and a section of the men, felt very
strongly that *OZ* was a sexist magazine, and shouldn't be given
uncritical support. Other gay men insisted that the *OZ* editors
had promised to change their policy and stop exploiting women,
etc., but the anti-sexist wing of GLF refused support except in
exchange for real guarantees, which were not forthcoming.

This incident showed the increasing influence of radical feminist
ideas from across the Atlantic, on many gay men as well as on the
lesbians. If it had been a great change in consciousness for us to
develop a new gay pride, it was a further leap forward to see our
particular problem as homosexuals as a direct function of something much bigger, the gender system of masculine and feminine,
which the women's liberation movement was in struggle against,
and which was the underlying cause of our oppression as homosexuals, as it was this that defined us as 'deviant'.

One of the results of the January 1971 think-in had been the
setting up of a Research and Discovery Group. Out of this there
soon emerged a Manifesto Group, whose aim was to write a
manifesto which would explain why gay people were oppressed

and map out the way forward to liberation. Like other key 'functional' groups of GLF, the Manifesto Group was influenced by the new radical feminism, and found the ideas of writers like Shulamith Firestone an immense help in its work. The Manifesto Group, made up of women and men, worked in a genuinely collective way throughout the spring and summer, discussing, researching, writing, etc. until the final *Manifesto* was published in October. This *Manifesto* has had a great influence over the years and must have sold at least 10,000 copies.

The London GLF *Manifesto* was a considerable advance on the earlier Principles. It represented a major attempt to integrate a theory of homosexual oppression into the general theory of society, and located the root cause of our oppression in the gender system. It pointed the way to a real synthesis between radical feminism and marxism, even though it has been pointedly ignored by all so-called marxists and left groups ever since it first came out, perhaps because its language was not rarified and obtuse enough – it was deliberately written in a style that could be understood by the non-university educated, i.e. the vast mass of homosexuals.

The *Manifesto* drew attention to a number of main ideas. A major starting-point of its analysis was its recognition that an individual's sexual orientation is determined by socio-cultural forces and not by biology. The reason why gay people are oppressed in so many societies is basically because we deviate from the gender system of masculine and feminine. This gender system is a cultural way of dealing with the biological base of male and female, and with species reproduction. Modern advances in contraception and infant mortality (the 2-pregnancy revolution) mean that the gender division is becoming increasingly archaic and therefore increasingly under attack. The contemporary women's movement also aims to abolish the gender division, as women are oppressed by the male domination that this enshrines. As the liberation of gay people and of homosexuality is only possible in the context of the breakdown of this system, the gay movement must therefore ally itself with the women's movement if it is to achieve this goal.

For the struggle of gay men and lesbians requires much more than just a civil rights campaign. It also requires a vigorous cultural struggle against the gender system and the family structure which supports it. The gay movement should link up with the attempts made in the women's movement and elsewhere to construct real alternatives to the family such as communes and living collectives, in which children are reared in a non-sexist and gender-free way. In other words, gay people should play a leading role in the construction of a gender-free zone, a no-go area for patriarchal domination.

While the *Manifesto* saw that the gender system is interlocked with the class system, so that women's and gay liberation must go together with the abolition of exploitative class society, it also stated quite clearly that class and sexual oppression are two different things. One is based on production, the other on pro-creation – and neither is reducible to the other.

When the *Manifesto* was put to the general meeting of London GLF, it was overwhelmingly acclaimed, and was actually studied and used throughout the movement. It gave gay liberationists a new weapon with which to struggle against ideological and political opponents. Yet the publication of the *Manifesto* was also the signal for a backlash against the characteristic radical ideas that GLF had developed. Within only a few weeks, the expansive euphoria that had marked the whole of 1971 was dampened by the first of a series of bitter and damaging splits, and the collapse of GLF had begun.

Interestingly enough, the first expression of this backlash came not from the large numbers of GLF supporters who did not fully understand or share the radical goals of the *Manifesto*, but rather from self-defined marxists who claimed to share the same goals. Unlike the women's movement, which was the open object of takeover attempts by various marxist 'vanguards', gay liberation was spared outright invasion by the trotskyist and other grouplets. Happily, these still found it far too embarrassing even to have to think about homosexuality. Right through the peak of London GLF's activity, for example, while many of our actions were reported in the Fleet Street press, the marxist journals studiously ignored us altogether. It was only the least traditional of the marxist groups that could orient themselves in any way towards the gay movement, as the Black Panther Party had bravely done in the United States. In Britain, this meant the circles around the Angry Brigade, a rather amateurish terrorist group that sought to copy the tactics of the Weathermen in the United States. But small though they were, these people did not stop at just giving support to gay liberation, which would have been very welcome, but typically sought to infiltrate our movement and use it for their own purposes.

Almost since the beginning of GLF, the Angry Brigade had been secretly attempting to recruit individual gay men and lesbians.

They also saw GLF with its various avenues into the clandestine network of gay society as a possible means for their activists to go underground. There was talk of setting up a specifically gay wing of the Angry Brigade. Early in 1971, several of us who firmly opposed any such attempts to hijack the gay movement had to work hard to block these moves. On the other hand, many people in GLF did cheer the bombings of the Angry Brigade, and saw its actions as expressing their own righteous frustration and anger at a system that denied them the right to exist as gay people.

In summer 1971, the police arrested eight people on terrorist and conspiracy charges, the Stoke Newington Eight. Four were later found guilty and imprisoned, four others acquitted, including Angela Weir, an active member of GLF. During the months that Angela spent, first in hiding, then in prison, then out on bail awaiting trial, sympathy with her naturally ran very deep in GLF, and it was this that the supporters of the Angry Brigade now tried to capitalise on.

About two weeks after the adoption of the GLF *Manifesto*, an article was submitted to Media Workshop, for publication in *Come Together*, by certain persons prominent in the Stoke Newington Eight defence campaign. This article, titled 'Towards a Revolutionary Gay Liberation Front', directly attacked the *Manifesto* and argued that GLF had become increasingly myopic in focussing too exclusively on the specifics of gay oppression and the struggle against sexism. It accused the majority of people in GLF of being gay chauvinist and neglectful of other oppressed communities in society – this despite the fact that GLF was constantly going on demonstrations supporting other issues, without this solidarity ever once being reciprocated! Media Workshop could only see this as yet another move to harness GLF to the purposes of the Angry Brigade.

In his book *Coming Out*, published in 1977, Jeffrey Weeks claims that Media Workshop rejected the article on 'spurious grounds', as it was 'moving rapidly towards a form of radical feminism' (p. 266). In fact, in the GLF vocabulary of the time, 'radical feminism' never meant a rejection of class struggle, but simply that a radical transformation of sexual relations was necessary, as well as a radical transformation of class relations. The GLF *Manifesto* was itself 'radical feminist' in these terms, and Media Workshop was in no way going against the general development of GLF, but precisely defending the positions of the *Manifesto* that had been so recently and overwhelmingly adopted.

What is more, Media Workshop was very far from imposing any kind of authoritarian censorship. We had sometimes had to reject articles before, and when we did so we always explained our reasons in full (see 'About *OZ*. About GLF. About Freedom' in *Come Together* 8). Despite the aggressive and anti-GLF tone of this article, we did not even reject it out of hand, but made constructive criticisms and asked for it to be rewritten in this spirit. It was then submitted again, still in a quite unsatisfactory form, and again rejected, despite the fact that its supporters tried to pack the Media Workshop meeting. Again contrary to what Jeffrey Weeks maintains (p. 199), there was no split among the regular Media Workshop activists. And Jeffrey omits to mention that, on Media Workshop's own suggestion, the article was duplicated in several hundred copies, and given out to everyone attending the general meeting, which was then asked to either endorse or overrule Media Workshop's decision. The article was thus made available to everyone involved in GLF, i.e. the people that it was addressing, and Media Workshop's decision met with overwhelming approval.

These may seem petty details, but this was the first of the splits that broke up GLF, a split among the radicals themselves, which prevented us from working together in the bigger storms that erupted soon after. And as always happens when people resort to terrorism, it becomes impossible to discuss certain important questions openly, and history gets distorted. Even six years later, Jeffrey Weeks could still imply that the Angry Brigade activities had nothing to do with GLF, and that the trial of the Stoke Newington Eight was simply 'a harsh clampdown on the political fringe' (p. 206). This split was in no way between 'socialists' and 'radical feminists' (p. 266), but rather between an alliance of dogmatists and terrorists who wanted to squeeze the new movements of women's and gay liberation into the traditional recipes for social revolution, and those of us who saw marxism as a structure of ideas that had to develop together with the real movement if it was to remain useful.

Women and Men

Very soon after the establishment of GLF, tensions began to emerge between the needs of lesbians and gay men. There were always many more gay men than lesbians in GLF, which was simply a reflection of the gay scene in general. At that time lesbians tended to keep a much lower social profile, due perhaps to their double oppression as women and as homosexuals.

Lesbianism had not yet become an issue in the women's movement, which was also still dominated organisationally by a few straight left groups. Most lesbians felt unable to come out in the women's movement. In fact it was almost a year before they managed to raise the question of lesbianism in a big way, as reported in the article on the Skegness conference of October 1971 in *Come Together* 10.

Although the GLF actions at the Gateways club were among the first of our demonstrations, on the whole lesbian issues were not given their due prominence. On top of the numerical predominance of men, many of these still maintained very chauvinist and condescending attitudes towards women. Of course this tendency was constantly struggled against, both by lesbians and by the large numbers of gay men who developed a feminist consciousness. A separate Women's Group was formed early on, though women continued to be active also in the functional groups, all of these – except the awareness groups – being mixed.

One typical example of male chauvinism and insensitivity to women which Media Workshop committed was the cover of *Come Together* 4, which portrayed a lesbian coming-out scene. Many women in GLF were absolutely furious about this cover, and Media Workshop was forced to print an apology to the sisters in the next issue – even though there were several women in Media Workshop who did not object to the cover at the time.

The two women's issues of *Come Together*, numbers 7 and 11, illustrate how the spread of feminist ideas took different forms among the GLF women, just as it did among the men. Issue 7 reflects a greater orientation towards class struggle, and some articles in it even play down the specific oppression of gay people. Issue 11, on the other hand, was put together by the Faraday Road collective, a commune whose operation is itself described in one article, and is oriented much more to the development of alternative lifestyles. The contradiction between women and men did not just put women on one side and men on the other. There were many cross-currents at work as well, as shown for example in Carla's article 'Want a Token Sister, Mister?' in *Come Together* 10.

The big actions that marked the peak of London GLF were all relevant to both lesbians and gay men, and were supported fully by the lesbians in GLF. For example the campaign against David Reuben's book, the struggles against the Festival of Light, and the resistance to the Notting Hill police and publicans. In the autumn of 1971, however, many lesbians were turned off by the growing concern of GLF with the all-male issue of cottaging, and with the unproductive ego-tripping of the general meetings. As feminist consciousness developed, they understandably had decreasing patience for dealing with the chauvinism of many gay men.

The parting of the ways was perhaps inevitable, once lesbians had gained some acceptance in the women's movement. Whereas at the start of GLF most of the lesbians involved had no experience of the women's movement and saw themselves as gay first and women second, this situation was unquestionably lop-sided and could not last in the long run. Separation was absolutely necessary, if lesbians and gay men were to relate in the future on an equal footing. It was formalised in February 1972. *

The contradiction between women and men in GLF did have a positive result, therefore, in that it left the women free to get on with their own politics, without being encumbered by the problems of the men. Among the GLF men, however, the question of male supremacy wreaked complete havoc, and blew the movement apart.

One of the stormiest of the all-London weekly meetings in Powis Square was in February 1972, when the women's GLF explained their reasons for splitting away, and requested half the GLF funds. The male chauvinism of a large number of men, and their complete failure to understand the contradiction between the sexes, was shown by the outright opposition to this request from a small minority of the men, and by the patronising response of a somewhat larger minority that the women should be given all the money. It took quite a struggle to convince the majority of the men that the women should have half the money, because that was what they had decided was fair. But the bitterness and antagonism that came to a head at meetings such as this one was not just between women and men; it was most extreme between feminists and anti-feminists in the men's GLF.

The issue was over the basic direction that the men's GLF should take, to continue the struggle against gender and therefore against male privilege, or to take the road of gay activism, as a purely civil-rights movement. Lined up in this struggle were, on

---

* The impact of the very just critique of male chauvinism made by the women at this time was confused by the actions of the Transvestites and Transsexuals group, who insisted that they were doubly oppressed within GLF, by the women as well as by the men. One transsexual actually handed round photos at the meeting of himself with both male genitals and breasts. From the feminist point of view, they were simply playing the game of the chauvinist men.

the one hand, the radical queens and a small number of marxist-feminists, backed by a good many men who had identified with the GLF *Manifesto* in a more general way. On the other hand, there were those who were trying to be very butch and man-identified, and those who simply took their male privilege for granted. Of course, very many men in GLF, perhaps the majority, fell somewhere in between these two extremes.

From the controversy over 'Towards a Revolutionary Gay Liberation Front' in November 1971, through to the suspension of the all-London weekly meetings in April 1972, these large general meetings, still attracting several hundred people, became real ideological battle-grounds. As a protest against the macho males, many would follow the lead of the radical queens and turn up to the meetings in straight women's clothes, or semi-drag, and would pointedly sit knitting and chatting through some person's big ego-trip speech. They would laugh and ridicule every sort of macho posturing, and this made some of the 'men' very insecure and very angry. Fierce arguments and screaming matches would continually break out. Many queens, who for years had felt that they were just little 'feathers' or 'clouds', would suddenly find that they had some really fine arguments against those butch macho gays who had always put them down as being bird-brained and presenting a bad image.

The *Manifesto* had turned out to be a great weapon, and had strengthened the hand of the radical queens. 'Butch really *is* bad', the *Manifesto* said, 'the oppression of others is an essential part of the masculine gender role'.* Ever since the beginning of GLF, the more conscious fem gays had been attacking those gay men who were into their male privilege, 'proud' of being men, and who were not in the slightest bit interested in changing the social position of the sexes. Fem gay men were the first to identify with the women's liberation movement and its struggles. They did this from the position of being psychically and emotionally more woman-identified than man-identified. Fem gay men have generally formed a stronger bond of identification with their mothers than with their fathers. This could be viewed as a plot by the female sex to emasculate the male sex, and was in fact seen in this very positive light by many people in GLF. Fem gay men and queens were definitely seen as a fifth column in the male sex, working to undermine its privilege and masculinity.

With the success of the campaign against the Festival of Light (led by the main focus of radical-queen activity, the Street

* p. 9 in the 1979 edition.

Theatre), and newly armed with the *Manifesto*, the radical queens had a field day. The meetings became ever more verbally violent and abusive, as well as extremely exhilarating and stimulating: 'You've got to have destruction, darling, before you can have a new fem reconstruction.' In no way, however, was the violence of the radical queens unprovoked. There was at least a substantial minority of gay men whose attachment to male privilege was complete and grotesque, summed up on one memorable occasion when one of the most active members of GLF from its earliest days stood up and proclaimed: 'I'll fuck anything, man, woman or dog!'

The problem of how to implement the *Manifesto*'s ideas in practice, however, was very difficult. How precisely were gay men to give up their male privilege? How could the gay movement link up with the women's movement? Although we were aware of our material privilege over women, because we were not in the one-to-one man/woman relationship of heterosexuality we did not have this concrete terrain for anti-sexist struggle. On the other hand, given the way that gay men have been violently persecuted, most men in GLF very understandably focussed on the immediate forms of their oppression. They wanted better social facilities and a wider space to do their thing; at most, they wanted to make sure that they would never again be sent to concentration camps, or burnt as faggots, or spied upon and imprisoned for having sex in ways not authorised by the law. The radical queens, however, thought that the way to link up with the women's movement was to eschew everything 'male'. They argued that gay men should give up their male privilege materially, for a start by giving up their privileged male jobs. They should then experience what it was like doing traditional women's work, such as housework, child care, etc., or go on Social Security and experience a leisured poverty and so put time and energy into changing their personalities, into becoming more receptive and sensitive to the needs of others. It was also felt necessary to show the world that you were giving up being a man, and this is where drag came in – it was a visible sign of what you were into.

Local Groups

The formation of local groups was in many ways a response to the increasingly destructive atmosphere of the all-London meetings. The first of these was started in Camden, North London, in November 1971. There was quite a bit of opposition to these local groups at first, as it was felt that they would divide GLF into powerless little sections, unable to do anything constructive or together. Some radicals also feared that the local groups would provide a refuge from feminist criticism for the more male chauvinist men. In fact, these local groups were only reflecting the genuine felt needs of the GLF membership, who increasingly could not relate to the all-London meetings. The more constructive atmosphere of the local groups liberated the pent-up energy of many people, and resulted in a whole new wave of innovative activities, such as Camden's midnight coffee stall on the Hampstead Heath cruising ground.

The local groups became the focus for different types of activity. Notting Hill, for example, was the centre for those into radical drag, while Camden became the focus for a soft-male image and for the marxist-feminists. West London was understandably closer to the gay ghetto, and South London had a more working-class orientation. There was however still mingling and mixing between different groups, as well as argument and struggle between them, even after the all-London meetings were discontinued in April 1972. The groups would often support each other's activities, and people from different groups would do the rounds of the local meetings. West London's weekly disco became an all-London GLF focus. And naturally many activities demanded cooperation if they were to be in any way successful, such as the Gay Pride week in June 1972, or participation on broad left demos such as that against the US war in Indochina in September. As London GLF split into local groups, the office became increasingly important as a coordinating centre. It continued to produce a very useful weekly newssheet. But with the end of the all-London meetings, the local groups increasingly went their separate ways.

In the spring and summer of 1972, the radical queens and the marxist-feminists, who had struggled together against male chauvinism at the all-London meetings, came into increasing conflict. The radical queen communards from Notting Hill would sweep into meetings and demand that people get into drag and make-up, haranguing anyone whom they considered too much of a 'man'. This sort of tactic had the opposite effect from what was intended, as it often drove gays back into their little butch moulds. Many men were also terrorised into bizarre and unproductive forms of drag.

The Camden approach was rather more subtle. We agreed with the radical queens on the importance of personal liberation, and like them saw gay men as torn between the privilege they are given if they conform to the male role, and their own inner needs that this represses; but we didn't see the answer as simply putting on a frock, let alone at ideological gun-point. We tried rather to develop an attractive alternative lifestyle that could win over the majority of gay men, stressing Gay Days, awareness groups and communes, getting over male hang-ups, with drag and make-up being only one possible aid in this process. Besides, it was clear that the feminism of the radical queens all too often didn't extend to coping with the traditional shit-work that women have been lumbered with — to give a mundane example, such tasks as making tea and washing up at our own meetings. The 'frock brigade's love of dressing up seemed to many of us to indicate the desire to have their cake and eat it too, to experience the 'glamour' that at least some women are able to cultivate, without the everyday oppression.

By summer 1972, however, it was becoming clear that GLF as a coherent radical movement had not survived the suspension of the all-London meetings, and that the gay movement was beginning to take a far more diffuse form. Both radical queens and marxist-feminists were now increasingly isolated minorities without any mass support. Each could continue their characteristic activities for a while, but before 1972 came to a close, the context of these activities had significantly changed. The heady days of GLF were over.

The fate of *Come Together* reflected the general development of GLF. Media Workshop continued to produce the paper almost monthly until issue 10 (November 1971), after which there was a general feeling that its production should circulate more. Four issues followed quite rapidly in the first six months or so of 1972: a lesbian issue, an issue produced by the office collective, one from Camden GLF and one from Birmingham GLF. Then there was a break of six months, before the Notting Hill issue in the new year of 1973, and finally an issue from Manchester in the summer. By this time there was virtually nothing left of London GLF, and the task of producing an issue of *Come Together* was quite daunting for most GLF groups outside of London. Leeds GLF planned to produce an issue 17, for autumn 1973, but were overwhelmed by work of their own.

Conclusion

In every city where GLF took root, it tended to follow a broadly similar trajectory, as a result of its internal dynamic and contradictions. The rise and fall of London GLF took place a year or so behind the major cities in the United States, and in other British cities the process was repeated some six to twelve months behind London. Naturally, in the smaller centres, people involved in the gay movement had to stick together that much more closely, and this often meant that the different tendencies within GLF did not separate out so clearly. In this Introduction, I've written from my own experiences in London GLF, particularly as *Come Together* was produced in London for all but two issues. I'm only too aware, however, that this was just one piece in the GLF kaleidoscope.

The rapid decline of GLF, as fast as its original rise, was above all a function of its own success. Not that the radical goals of the GLF *Manifesto* had been achieved, or even more than a tiny bit of progress made towards them. Even the immediate GLF Demands still have a good way to go before they are met. But in two years of militant campaigning and consciousness-raising, GLF certainly did manage to expand quite significantly the social space open to gay men and lesbians in the present society.

When we started London GLF in October 1970, we certainly didn't expect our aims to be achieved overnight. Quite the contrary. We saw gay liberation as a revolutionary movement, which challenged the existing society in a quite fundamental way, and expected we would meet with violent resistance from the state and other apparatuses of repression. Even such modest steps as holding public gay dances, we anticipated, might lead to major clashes with the forces of law and order. We were surprised, looking back after a couple of years, that without any structural change in the sexist and capitalist society, this had managed to grant certain concessions that made life a lot more confortable, at least for the minority of homosexuals who actually come out and live an openly gay lifestyle. Naturally, this was far more so in London than elsewhere.

The immediate achievement of GLF was to have led the advance from the traditional gay ghetto, very confined and re-pressed, to a somewhat less inhibited gay community. After GLF had blazed this trail, the gay community ramified in many different directions. A great deal of the new infrastructure involved the encroachment of commercial interests: new clubs, the big discos, as well as dating services, hotels, travel agencies, etc. What is more important, though, is the great expansion of community services run by gay people for gay people on a non-profit basis: telephone lines, counselling services, self-help groups of all kinds for young gays, elderly gays, disabled gays, etc. as well as a great variety of special interest groups. Many institutions of the gay community today had their roots directly in London GLF. The Icebreakers counselling service grew out of the GLF Counter-Psychiatry Group, Gay Switchboard out of the office collective, *Gay News* from people involved in the GLF Action Group, and so on.

GLF broke down one of the barriers that hem gay people in, and confine us to the margins of society. Beyond this barrier there are a whole series of others, but compared to the nightmare world of the past, the expansion of the ghetto can well seem like real liberation. Once our space was widened in this way, the many gays who had followed GLF, and even come to share its radical rhetoric, no longer needed this radicalism, and those small groups that still tried to make a stand for the ideas of the GLF *Manifesto* were left high and dry. This isn't to say that the political consciousness that GLF developed has completely disappeared. There is still a section of politicised gays prepared both to campaign for immediate demands and to support longer-term perspectives. Something of the old GLF spirit survives, in fragmented ways, in organisations such as GAA, in magazines such as *Outcome*, and in some of the gay squats and communes, and it's significant that the 1971 GLF *Manifesto* still goes on selling. Yet since the demise of GLF, gay people have not *come together* again as a revolutionary force able to tilt a bit further the balance of social relations. The separate struggles of the late 1970s have been more to defend and consolidate positions already won, rather than actually breaking new ground. And yet to see how little has actually been achieved, we need only glance at the original GLF Demands, very modest in comparison with the radical feminist goals that later developed.

There is still vicious 'discrimination by the law, by employers, and by society at large', there is still police harassment, and too many psychiatrists still treat homosexuality as a sickness, even if certain progress has been made on these fronts. The age of consent for gay males remains 21, and even the 1967 Act hasn't been extended to Scotland and Northern Ireland. Sex education in schools is still as good as exclusively heterosexual. And there is a very long way indeed to go before 'all people who feel attracted to a member of their own sex be taught that such feelings are perfectly valid'.

Perhaps the most striking indication of how little has changed comes from studying the last demand, 'that gay people be free to hold hands and kiss in public, as are heterosexuals'. How often do we feel able to express ourselves in a natural way, on the streets, in parks, swimming pools, on the beach, wherever we might happen to be? How often do we express ourselves freely even before the more limited 'public' of our own families? We are actually less free to do so today than we were in the time of GLF, when we felt the support of a strong mass movement behind us, inspiring us with its warmth and solidarity. This shows all too clearly how we are still forced to live on the margins of society. The ghetto has been gilded, but we should not deceive ourselves that this is liberation.

But a more far-reaching achievement of GLF than the expansion of our immediate social space may well be the contribution it has made to revolutionary theory, widening the possibilities open to humanity in its further development as a species.

At the turn of the 1970s, the gay liberation movement worked convergently with the women's movement to put in question the gender system. The specific contribution of gay liberation was to challenge for the first time the primacy of heterosexuality, which the earliest radical feminist ideas had not yet done. Even Shulamith Firestone, in her *Dialectic of Sex*, maintained that after the gender system was overthrown, heterosexuality would still be the norm, as it was 'more convenient' — for whom may we ask?

For the first time in human history, the vision of a gender-free society began to emerge — one where it would be possible for male and female human beings to be neither masculine nor feminine, but to combine the positive attributes of both genders and dispense with the negative ones. GLF vigorously maintained that homosexuality was definitely superior to heterosexuality as a form of sexuality and basis for human relationships at this present time in human history, when the balance of power between female and male is still so uneven. Gay showed the way out of the gender trap. A gender-free society will represent a genuine qualitative leap forward in our social evolution towards a more just and egalitarian future. And from the idea of the elimination of gender it became possible to conceive of a future time when humans would be able to overcome even their biological division into two sexes. When human procreation becomes extra-uterine within a gender-free society of full equality between females and males, it will be possible to reproduce ourselves as beings with no particularly determinant sex, beings who will transcend the male-female divide altogether. The jump out of the womb into the test-tube will be our next major biological leap forward as a species. This development may of course be forced upon us by the increasing release of radioactivity into the natural environment resulting in damage to the human gene pool. But whether it takes place from force of circumstances, or whatever, it will necessarily free women from the tyranny of biology and in itself completely negate heterosexual reproductive activity.

The second major biological leap, stemming from the first, will be even more significant for us as it will mean the complete transformation of humans from being a sexed species, like our lower animal relatives, into a higher non-sexed species. It will also mean the complete separation of orgasmic capacity and potential from the confines of a system based on sexual reproduction. What the chromosomal base will be for this evolutionary step, whether it will mean the eradication of the XY and XX in favour of XO or something (the mind boggles), must be left to future generations to decide.

Such ideas could only have emerged from the gay and lesbian movements, because heterosexuals have so much of their identities tied up in the gender division and with reproduction. It is no valid objection to point out that gender games are very far from dead in the gay male and lesbian communities. The point is that up till now, the social norm has been *hetero-sexual*, i.e. sexuality has been essentially a relationship between unlike and unequal individuals, and this poisonous regime has to a certain — if lesser — extent affected even relationships between people of the same sex. Gay liberation proclaims that the social norm should be *homo-sexual*, i.e. that sexuality should be a relationship between like and equal individuals, and that this principle, which has its origin in relations between people of the same sex, should be extended to all sexual relations.

A gender-free society may appear an impossible dream from the vantage-point of the heterosexist tyranny we still live under, but it has already taken root in the minds and practices of many people. Even if these are so far still a minority, it is a minority with vision, and hence influence. As new generations come up against gender tyranny, they will have examples to follow, and will not have to break completely new ground.

The gay liberation movement was not simply a 'last major product of late 1960s euphoria', as Jeffrey Weeks suggests in *Coming Out* (p.206). This is completely to belittle what was radically new in GLF in comparison with all previous movements of homosexuals. The objective reasons behind both women's and gay liberation lie rather in the acute crisis of the gender system. This may well have had its place in Earth's history, enabling the human race to expand and develop (though through the exploitation and enslavement of women), but it has now turned into its opposite, and become an insidious burden. Firstly, the way that it ties sexuality to procreation is quite intolerable, now that our planet has been amply populated, and population control is a basic necessity of survival. Yet despite all the scientific technologies applied to birth control, vast numbers of unplanned and unwanted children are still being born in every country of the world, including our own, as a result of heterosexual activity. Homosexuality cannot be *the* solution to the population problem, but there will never be any solution to this problem unless homosexuality is completely liberated.

Secondly, the gender system involves the complete subjugation and oppression of women. All over Earth it has used such things as footbinding, rape, clitoridectomy, *suti* (the burning of widows), witch burning, terror, etc. to achieve this subjugation. If the relative reduction in the burden of child-bearing has enabled feminists to set as their goal the complete breakdown of the gender system, the gay contribution has a vital part to play in the struggle for this goal, in challenging the established definitions of masculine and feminine.

Thirdly, the gender system as we know it today is inextricably bound up with other dimensions of oppression, in particular the class system, with its exploitation, violence and war, and the escalating destruction of our planetary environment in the name of 'production'. With the development of class societies, masculinity came to be ever more identified with competitive self-assertion and the readiness to use violence, against both other human beings and the rest of the biosphere, as the basic way of resolving contradictions. Today with the growing threats of nuclear war and ecocide hanging so closely over us, we simply cannot afford to continue in the same old way. We must struggle to completely overcome and eradicate this ancient masculine aggressive hunting-type mentality, both in our own heads and in its social manifestations. Instead we should encourage a mentality of nurture — or caring — for Earth and for each other. After all, what else do we have apart from our planet and our fellow humans?

If we don't manage a radical change of direction, we shall fail to survive, and other more successful galactic cultures will look back and say: 'Oh, Earth? That died out eons ago! It's a shame, there were too many factors working against intelligent life, too much testosterone in the planet's crust'.

So if Gay Liberation Front was only a little ripple, the ideas generated at that time have a very great future ahead of them. History never repeats itself; we should not look back to the 'good old days' and expect a similar movement to come round again. Certainly, the generation of lesbians and gay men who have grown up in the post-GLF period will initiate a new phase of radicalism, as they can no longer be lulled by comparing the bad situation of gay people today with the far worse situation of the past. And the spirit of gay liberation is still very much swirling around the planet, settling in countries where the time is ripe to battle against the vicious gender system, such as Spain, Mexico and Brazil. Yet people who come to understand the ideas of gay liberation today can less then ever confine themselves simply to the specific problems of the gay minority. The gender system that oppresses us is such a central element in the present social disorder, that there can be no gay liberation that is not an aspect of a general human liberation. The challenge facing us now is to incorporate our particular perspective into the general struggle for a qualitatively new society that is increasingly urgent if human life on this planet is to survive and go forward.

Aubrey Walter

London, July 1980

Come Together was the newspaper of a movement, and produced by a collective. Hardly anyone in Media Workshop or the other groups that produced issues of the paper had professional or academic skills. We had to learn as we went along. In many of the articles there were a lot of typing errors, rather crazy punctuation, and occasionally a word or two missing. I've set out to reproduce all articles as closely as possible to the original, and made only the minimal changes in spelling, punctuation, etc. needed to make them readable.

It was part of the spirit of GLF that people rarely signed articles with their full names. Many articles were unsigned, many were written collectively, many just had the first names of their writers, and some writers gave pseudonyms. I've made no attempt to establish who were the 'real' writers of these articles, even in those cases where I remember this information. They are all attributed just as they were in the original.

This anthology contains about half the articles that appeared in *Come Together*, rather more from some issues, rather less from others. Within the limits of size, I have tried to include pieces that reflect all the main ideas and aspects of GLF. Only two of these articles were reprints from other journals: Steve Dansky's 'Hey Man', from the New York *Come Out*, and Rachel Pollack's 'The Twilight World of the Heterosexual', from the short-lived London magazine *Ink*.

Cover of *Come Together* 6; GLF on the anti-IRB demo (February 1971)

Come Together
1

[*November 1970*]

Who We Are

This broadsheet has been put together by a small collective of gay sisters and brothers in the Media Workshop group of GLF. We by no means represent the opinions of all the GLF members, but hope to be able to provide a service to all those of us who have something to say about the oppression that gay people suffer. We will also attempt to keep the gay community in touch with the activities of the Gay Liberation Front and any other attempts by sisters and brothers to put an end to the physical, psychological, economic and generally all-round oppression that they suffer. Poems, drawings and any other creative things done by our sisters and brothers will be included, though try to bear in mind that we don't really have that much space due to limited funds.

We would like to say right now that all the so-called gay mags, such as *Jeremy*, are just a load of absolute bullshit and an outright insult to gay people. They just try to foist a 'closet-queen' mentality onto us; they think that all we are interested in are the secret life of closet pseudostars and the latest in rip-off bourgeois fashions. Some of us are just about pissed-off with this shit and are beginning to say — 'No More! From now on gay people in Britain are going to write their own history'.

We're Coming Out Proud

We've probably all heard of the Louis Eakes case — the Young Liberal who was convicted of 'gross indecency' on Highbury Fields by the flimsiest of police 'evidence'. No doubt many gay people thought it was just another case of police harassment and something we're all powerless to do anything about. But at our meeting of over 200 last Wednesday (Nov. 25th), the sisters and brothers were seething with anger at this, the latest amongst hundreds of crimes committed against gay people by the police and the establishment every year. The fact that Eakes claims to be straight is beside the point, we were angry at the very fact that the police have the power to arrest and harass people on the slightest suspicion.

We therefore decided to protest the Eakes conviction by holding a 'gay-in' on Highbury Fields at ten on Friday evening after contacting the press and the police. So 150 beautiful gay people assembled outside Highbury and Islington station about nine o'clock; a few of us were talking to sensation-hungry reporters. We then proceeded to the scene of the 'crime' carrying and squeaking balloons, and shouting 'gay power' slogans. Assembling at the far end of the Fields we lit candles and torches, and listened to a brother reading our demands. After each demand we all responded with 'Right on!' which echoed around the Fields. Many of us felt that listening to our demands was not really strong enough and so decided to fulfil some of them there and then by holding each others' hands and kissing. Of course the photographers jumped to take pictures — and we let them, we had nothing to be ashamed of. At one point a brother overheard a bunch of straight, grey reporters describe us as a bunch of 'pooves'. So we descended on this bunch and demanded a retraction, and that they recognise our demands as just. Half of us then felt like demonstrating our power of togetherness by walking round the Fields arm in arm, kissing, shouting slogans, and with our torches, fists and heads held high.

Coming together again it was agreed that we'd demonstrated our point, and we all made our way back to the pub, stopping on the way to light each others' cigarettes (this was all that Eakes said he did).

The next day I rushed out to buy all the papers, thinking there would be banner headlines and 'sensational' pictures. But after spending about four bob all I could find was one very mild report in the *Times*. It looks as though there had been a press boycott because a truthful report would have encouraged our sisters and brothers in the provinces and suburbs to get into militant activity. The report in the *Times* deliberately played down the politics of our action, and made it appear as though we were being meek and mild like CHE. They did concede the point, however, that this was the first public demonstration by homosexuals in the history of these sceptered isles.

Right On to Gay Liberation.   Jonathan

Gay Local Government Hang-Up

I am a local government officer, typically surrounded at work by round, bald, friendly conservatives, severe career spinsters, 'dolly' local girls, dull straight boys. In this universe I am deviant in at least one visual way: I am one of the few wearers of post-1965 fashion in suits.

But there are no problems in being gay because I never talk about it. The round friendly conservatives tell me to look forward to the day when I shall be married with two kids. The spinsters surprise themselves to find that young men go places at weekends. The 'dolly' girls think I have a non-stop, rave, hetero time. The boys think I do the same as them. Banging a nice bit of crumpet, they say. I am, however, well-practised in evasion, negative lying and counter-conspiracies of silence — it works.

In so far as I am successful in looking younger than I am, I am lucky, as the junior office boy is invulnerable in his position of no responsibility. But I don't think I would get the sack if I told everybody — they wouldn't believe me.

It is very easy to get so used to this silent oppression that it ceases to be noticed or felt. It becomes increasingly difficult to join the oppression-smashers.

I think there must be a lot of gay local government officers who will be terrified of the Gay Liberation Front. But GLF is for everybody who wants solidarity against oppresion. So Come Out and join your sisters and brothers at GLF.

Local Government Officer

Our Demands Are . . .

1 — that all discrimination against gay people, male and female, by the law, by employers, and by society at large, should end.

2 — that all people who feel attracted to a member of their own sex be taught that such feelings are perfectly normal.

3 — that sex education in schools stop being exclusively heterosexual.

4 — that psychiatrists stop treating homosexuality as though it were a problem or sickness, thereby giving gay people senseless guilt complexes.

5 — that gay people be as legally free to contact other gay people, through newspaper ads, on the streets and by any other means they may want, as are heterosexuals, and that police harassment should cease right now.

6 — that employers should no longer be allowed to discriminate against anyone on account of their sexual preferences.

7 — that the age of consent for gay males be reduced to the same as for straights.

8 — that gay people be free to hold hands and kiss in public, as are heterosexuals.

GAY POWER TO GAY PEOPLE
ALL POWER TO OPPRESSED PEOPLE

Come Together
2

[December 1970]

*Principles**

1. GLF's first priority is to defend the immediate interests of gay people against discrimination and social oppression.
2. However, the roots of the oppression that gay people suffer run deep in our society, in particular to the structure of the family, patterns of socialisation, and the Judeo-Christian culture. Legal reform and education against prejudice, though possible and necessary, cannot be a permanent solution. While existing social structures remain, social prejudice and overt repression can always re-emerge.
3. GLF therefore sees itself as part of the wider movement aiming to abolish all forms of social oppression. It will work to ally itself with other oppressed groups while preserving its organisational independence.
4. In particular, we see these groups as including:
    a) The women's liberation movement. The roots of women's oppression are in many ways close to our own (see 2 above).
    b) Black people and other national minorities. The racism that these peoples are affected by has a similar structure of prejudice to our own, but on the basis of racial instead of sexual difference. They are socially and economically the most oppressed group in our society.
    c) The working class, i.e. all productive manual and mental workers. Their labour is what the whole of society lives off, but their skills are misused by the profit-oriented economy, and their right to organise and defend their interests is under increasing attack.
    d) Young people, who are rejecting the bourgeois family and the roles and lifestyles offered them by this society, and attempting to create a non-exploitative counterculture.

* The Principles were in fact printed in *Come Together* 4, not 2, but I've included them here as they're referred to in other articles and it was at this time that they were first adopted.

e) Peoples oppressed by imperialism, who lack the national political and economic independence which is a precondition for all other social change.

5. We don't believe that any existing revolutionary theory has all the answers to the problems facing us. GLF will therefore study and discuss all relevant critical theories of society and the individual being, to measure them against the test of our own and historical experience.

The Gay Liberation Front Adopts Principles

GLF has adopted a list of principles, or guidelines, and has recognised the need for a more cohesive organisational structure. We recognised that the oppression that gay people suffer is an integral part of the social structure of our society. Women and gay people are both victims of the cultural and ideological phenomenon known as sexism.

This is manifested in our culture as male supremacy and heterosexual chauvinism. Sexism is a recent concept developed by our sisters and brothers in the American women's and gay liberation movements. It is such an insidious thing that often its victims, women and gay people, are sexist in their attitudes towards themselves and their sisters and brothers. It is sexism that produces closet queens, the rigid exploitative butch and fem roles and the self-hatred that many gay people are into. Of course most straights are also into rigid sexist roles. In fact many sisters and brothers maintain that straight men are just as much victims of sexism as are women and gay people. This is true only in the sense that sexism limits their true potential as human beings. But at the same time they do have a vested interest in sexist roles; they often use women as mere chattels and sex objects, and use gay people as scapegoats for their own sexual hang-ups.

Many of you may be disturbed by the fact that in our principles we support the struggles of social groups who themselves are prejudiced and use sexism to put down gay people. However it is important to see that no one single revolutionary change in our social structure can be achieved without the whole system being changed. We should not confuse legal changes with real structural change. Legality can always at some point be changed to illegality (witness the present government's attack on the trade-union movement, and its legal attacks on the rights of coloured immigrants). The legalisation of public gay activity, though something we should strive for, will not really alter the fact that the deepest oppression of gay people is inflicted in the family, and is manifested in a gay person's psyche.

Gay activity is a direct threat to the existence of the nuclear family. Gay people in our Judeo-Christian culture have never been given a 'niche' as they have in many other cultures; they have always been regarded as pariahs and persecuted as such. The niche allotted to straight women has always been the family, in which hers has been the pivotal socialising role. Gay people, by their rejection of the nuclear family, threaten the very reproduction of the wider society. Hence their repression.

Periodically, capitalist nations in political and economic crisis have resorted to outright physical and ideological repression of the vast masses of the population. This classically takes the form of attacks on autonomous working-class organisation, the use of ethnic minorities as national scapegoats, and the enforcement of traditional familial, sexist roles (the woman in the home breeding babies and the man on the factory floor). Together with this idealisation of the traditional familial roles goes the open persecution of gay people. In Nazi Germany many tens of thousands of gay people met their deaths in the gas chambers of concentration camps. In the camps, Jews were given yellow stars to wear, homosexuals were given pink tags and other nationalities were given different coloured tags. Now it is a known fact that not one of the memorials to the concentration-camp victims say anything about our sisters and brothers who were butchered. The colours of the Jews and other nationalities and political victims are represented, but somehow the colour pink gets forgotten about. Does this mean that the people who erected the memorials think gay people deserve to be put to death for being gay, or what?

Why did I mention this? Could it happen here? Well, we can see that our government is carrying out racist policies towards our black sisters and brothers (the immigration acts, new pass laws etc.) and is in the process of putting through anti-working-class activity in the form of the IRB. Who will be the next victims of 'law and order'? Gay people, by their very existence, threaten hallowed social institutions and ideology. Perhaps it could be us... Hence the need for an independent Gay Liberation engaged in militant activity and lending its support to other sections in struggle. In return these other social sectors will lend us their support in our struggle.

The Gateways Club and Gay Liberation

As part of our leafleting effort last Saturday week three girls went to the Gateways, London's best-known lesbian club, to hand out publicity about the GLF dance. Two of us started to hand out leaflets — there was a lot of interest both in the movement as a whole and in the dance.

Suddenly as we were standing chatting, one of the women who run the club, known as Smithy, came up and snatched our leaflets from us.

A long argument ensued, as a result of which one of us was banned from the club for life. The other two were let off with a warning, because we are old and untroublesome members who have never necked in the lavatories or knocked anyone out, and also because it was our first offence so far as distributing GLF literature was concerned.

The interesting thing about the argument however was the attitude of the proprietors — themselves a lesbian couple of at least ten years' standing. I was talking throughout to Smithy, the 'butch' one, but I gather her friend was saying more or less the same things.

Smithy's attitude is that they object to GLF leaflets because they are opposed to GLF aims and don't wish to be associated with our movement, but it went much further than this. Smithy said:

'When you come down to it, we *are* abnormal. We're a minority... I think everything is beautiful the way it is — we have a lot of freedom — two girls can walk down the street hand in hand if they want to. No, I *don't* think men should be allowed to hold hands and kiss in public, I think that's *disgusting* — men! — do you know why we won't have men down here? Because whenever we do, if you go out to the toilets you'll find two men out there having a quick bash, and the next moment they're doing it with a girl — they just don't care what they have, it's just quick sex, they can't have relationships, it's disgusting...

'I *don't* think the age of consent should be the same for men — men are supposed to be three years behind girls anyway, aren't they? Do *you* think it should be legal for an old man to seduce a sixteen-year-old boy? I don't... well, I don't think a sixty-year-old woman should seduce a young girl either — would you like it if that happened to your sixteen-year-old sister? And I don't believe it's legal either — no, it is not legal.'

(There followed an argument about what the age of consent is, Smithy convincing herself more and more firmly that it is eighteen. When all other arguments failed she flexed her muscles and said, 'Well, I'm a bigger lesbian than either of you will ever be.')

She continued: 'I'm opposed to your aims because I don't think changing the law can alter attitudes. You won't change *anything*, baby — no you will not. You want to force it down people's throats . . . you want to change everything — the whole of society — but you won't — no — because people don't want to change — things are all right the way they are . . . I think the whole idea of kissing in public is horrible — why can't you do it at home, in privacy? If you have a steady girlfriend you don't *need* to kiss in the streets. Why parade yourselves?

'You think you're going to change the world, love, but let me tell you all you're going to do is bring people down on us and we'll all end up worse off. That's all you're going to do.'

Although we tried to argue with her it was obvious that she simply could not listen or take in anything we said — that's how rooted her attitudes are. The really sad thing is her negative attitude to her own lesbianism; she came back many times to the statement 'We *are* abnormal.' I would include as part of her negative attitude and distorted self-image the rigidly sex-defined roles she and her girlfriend feel compelled to play — 'butch' and 'femme', as among the most traditionalist heterosexual couples. This is not a personal attack, but it is another indication of the unliberated state of this as of very many other lesbian couples in which one partner plays the submissive 'feminine' role, as exploited as many married women.

I don't think the Gateways management intends to exploit lesbians, but on the contrary believe they provide a relatively pleasant and unsordid locale in which lesbians can meet, talk and dance.

But what is to be done about attitudes like this?

Elizabeth

Homosexuality and Therapy

Most of us are in the fortunate position whereby we can fight for freedom from oppression. Many of our brothers and sisters, however, are not even in a position to protest.

For instance, I remember only a few years ago, when I was working in a mental hospital, a young sixteen-year-old boy who had been committed to us by order of the Courts, was admitted to a locked ward, along with patients whom the hospital had found to be most disturbed or who were considered dangerous. When I asked about his diagnosis, I was told that he was 'another fucking queer'. Apparently he had been caught 'indulging in a homosexual relationship', and had previously been suspected of stealing some of his sister's clothes. Once in the hospital, he was subjected to the usual ridicule of the staff and was made to feel abjectly guilty and despicable. One of his daily tasks was to clean the ward lavatories, this presumably being considered suitable 'occupational therapy'. The patients were woken at 6 a.m., Sundays and Christmas included, and his first job was to clean the toilets. This is not an incredibly unusual situation!

We are nowadays told that we are 'sick' and in need of treatment. The treatment consists of breaking down the individual's pleasurable response to someone of the same sex that he/she might feel drawn to emotionally and physically, and substituting an aversion reaction.

This is achieved by means of electric shocks or emetic drugs, given when the patient responds favourably, so that the unpleasantness of being violently sick or receiving an electric shock is associated with the photograph of the desirable person. I would like to emphasise that in-patient psychiatric treatment and private psychiatry often differ radically. If one is able to enjoy the benefits of private help, emotional support and sustenance is very likely to be offered. I have not seen this occur often in mental hospital treatment regimes. There are, and indeed have been, very many ethical objections to the use of such a form of therapy. However, my main concern at this particular juncture is that the person who administers the emetic drug or electric shock, is almost invariably a psychiatric nurse. I object strongly to this situation for several reasons. Not the least of which is that this is destroying a potentially supportive relationship. One may reasonably ask why nurses let themselves become involved in a procedure such as aversion therapy. Why didn't some of the nurses object to the locking up of a sixteen-year-old boy in an adult disturbed ward? The majority of psychiatric nurses are men. To challenge, question, or protest about the treatment meted out to a homosexual patient, renders one 'suspect'. Men depend upon their jobs to earn a living, even men nurses. 'Suspected' men don't seem to get promotion, or alternatively seem to be prone to 'unsatisfactory' work records and are dismissed. In the same hospital, a colleague of mine, a young, skilled and compassionate ward sister, was dismissed when it was discovered that she was having a love affair with one of the female student nurses. (After all, she might assault the patients.) Doctors and nurses are subjected to statutory disciplinary committees. They are liable to be deprived of their livelihood if found to be homosexual, even if no illegal activity has occurred!

'The council have power to take disciplinary action against a registered nurse if it is brought to their attention (whether through the Courts, employing authorities, or individuals) that the nurse has been guilty of a felony, or misdemeanour, *or of any misconduct which warrants consideration as to whether her name should be removed from the register . . .' (Functions, Procedure and Disciplinary Jurisdiction of the GMC*, page 4).

What would you do? What *we* can, and must do, both for the protection of our brothers and sisters in the medical and nursing professions, and most important, for the patients, is this:

We must strengthen the position of the doctor or nurse, so that they will not be in a vulnerable position if they wish to object to 'treatment' policies. To achieve this, we must write to the appropriate statutory bodies and demand that no doctor or nurse be deprived of his/her livelihood because of their sexual orientation. [Names and addresses follow.]

We must write to the medical and nursing press and make point 4 of our manifesto [= GLF Demands] quite clear — that we stop being treated as 'sick' people. [Names and addresses follow.]

By changing the attitude of society at large, we will eventually modify the attitudes of potential medical and nursing students, and thus reduce the risk of patients being traumatised by psychiatric 'help'.

Martyn (a registered mental nurse)

What is a Homosexual?

Ok. So what *is* a homosexual in the eyes of the straight public? A flamboyant queen, limp wrists, fluttering hands, make-up, mincing steps, dyed hair, affected voice and lisping. Any one or combination of these and immediately you're a 'fucking queer'. And how are straights to know better?

Colourful articles such as appeared in the last issue of *Come*

Together covering the Highbury Fields thing are not going to help any — neither in the form of description nor the activities described — i.e. holding hands, kissing, arm in arm, etc. What is needed is to show that we are ordinary 'normal' people with the same thought-processes, interests, attitudes, politics and activities, no different from the straights themselves, except in one preference. Anyone stumbling on the last meeting of GLF (2nd Dec.) would have found it hard to believe that the large group of heads, freaks, coloureds, chicks, etc. were almost 100 per cent homosexual.

There were many ideas for rallies, marches, demos put up, but what for? What against? And what a laughing stock if we held a meeting in Trafalgar Square or wherever for the vast gathering of three or four hundred. For demos wait until we're sure of thousands turning out not mere hundreds. Cool it, where's the rush? Same goes for 'Gay-Ins' in Hyde Park. (In this weather, yet!)

The culminative idea came at the end of a meeting from a girl called Sue. She really had the handle, and it was worth waiting through two hours of mainly bullshit for that one constructive suggestion. A group of two or three hundred outside a Fleet Street news office is *just* the thing to start with. A vast number of persons is not needed to attract attention (stop the traffic also). Doubtful if there would be papers *not* printing reports — it would be happening right on their territory. There is a specific person for focal point, and a specific article for fuel. There would be press men and photographers to show it wasn't a group of screaming queens, and to be surprised at the number of chicks there, and in one go GLF would have its advance publicity — and free at that.

It's very much up to young heads, etc. like me, who have little or nothing to lose, and are not ashamed, or afraid, or too proud, conceited or just plain lazy to show the straights that they are not so special by just being straight. I'm not fighting for, or prepared to fight for, the queens — they kill themselves (and everyone else) first time out. It's the others who count — the people the straights wouldn't believe were homosexual even if you pointed out that they sat next to them on the tube, worked at the next desk, ate supper with them, were driven in taxis, buses by them, even were related to them (and how can you *tell*?). And particularly the older people unable to do anything because of families, positions, children etc., but who would like, and need, to see the laws and attitudes changed.

Paul Daniel

GLF Street Theatre show some of the niceties of a do-it-yourself abortion (summer 1971).

Come Together
3

[January 1971]

Gay Liberation This Way?

Sisters and brothers, I feel I must reply to the last two articles in
Come Together 2, as they both seem to ask the same questions —
what is a homosexual and what is gay liberation for?* Both
articles put the same point of view, that homosexuals are the
same as anyone else and so no one need worry about us. But
surely that is exactly what we aren't, surely if we have learnt
anything from our oppression, it is that 'ordinary people' are
racist, sexist and oppressive. I don't want to be like Nixon or
Heath — they are 'ordinary people'.

Within the limits of space in this article I hope to show why
people, including ourselves, are oppressive in these ways, and
suggest directions that GLF might take in the struggle for
liberation.

An oppresssion started by the ruling class and purveyed through
every form of media at their disposal — schools, press, tv and
radio — has forced this oppression onto society as a whole, even
into the gay community. We have been forced into playing roles
based on straight society, butch and femme, nuclear 'marriages'
which continue within the relationship the same oppression that
outside society forces onto its women.

If we are to effectively combat this oppression we must isolate
our enemies and find our friends whom we can unite with. Our
primary enemy is the ruling class — the 5 per cent who own 90 per
cent of the wealth of this country. It is this ruling class which has
oppressed us and our straight sisters and brothers into the attitudes
of mind that we have. It is the same ruling class that oppresses
factory workers, office workers, women, black people and Irish
too. It is for those reasons that GLF must advance the slogan
'Workers and Oppressed People of the World Unite'. We must

---

* The articles were 'What Is a Homosexual?' , and 'World's First Gay
Community?', which isn't reprinted here. This article reported the attempt by
Californian gay liberationists to 'liberate' the remote and sparsely populated
Alpine county in the Sierra Nevada.

align ourselves with those in struggle against this monster, we must analyse our situation and discover who are the people who will support us and who are the enemy who will be against us regardless of our arguments. Straight people who oppress us, but who are themselves oppressed at work or because of their race or sex, can be won over to supporting us when the contradiction in their position is explained, but people who identify themselves with the ruling class in all respects are our enemy and must be treated as such. It is only by uniting with our supporters that we can liberate ourselves and others, for we can only be truly liberated in a liberated society — we will not be liberated until women are liberated, blacks are liberated, until the people have all the power.

We will not be liberated by refusing to support the 'screaming queens' who Paul puts down and will not fight for. They were the first people to come out and they have suffered for it. They are our first martyrs, and it is straight society we must indict for this — not the queens. Also we must not demand from the closet queens that they come out *now*. Certainly if we are to be liberated we must come out and closet queenery must end, but let's get our head clear on one thing. Closet queens are our brothers too, and must be defended from attacks by straights, but we who have come out must not force others to come out; the stakes are high and while closet queenery is part of our oppression, it's more a part of theirs, they alone can decide when and how.

As far as the gay community in Alpine county is concerned, I hope I have shown above that we cannot liberate ourselves by isolating ourselves from other people in struggle. Don Kilhefner says: 'We can't be honest in a society in which we have to hide our feelings. This way we can obey Nixon's injunction to work within the system'. Well, there comes a time, brother, when you have got to stop running and be honest or lose what little self-respect you have been allowed to keep, and as far as working within the system is concerned, the blacks in Amerika have tried it for centuries and have now been forced to pick up the gun to defend themselves against attacks from the police, whilst in Ireland the working class (both Protestant and Catholic) tried it and found that armed British troops were there to back up the state.

Let's stop running, get our heads clear as to where society is at and how we can best change it. Let's develop a theory of our oppression and seek the support of the people (it's there if you are honest about what you are), and I say let's realise that only by fighting for a socialist revolution can we succeed in being liberated.

All Power to the People!

Andy

GLF and Male Chauvinism

At the last meeting of GLF (Arts Lab, 30th Dec. 1970) there was a lot of discussion on whether there should be a separate women's caucus and whether they should meet. As I felt the women in the meeting were yet again dominated by the men in the debate on whether the men should be in on their discussions, I think that that example is in itself a good reason for the women talking on their own. I myself hopefully look forward to the emergence of a lesbian liberation voice. Unfortunately I feel bad about the fact that I'm a man putting forward a point that should be made by the women, but as was shown in the last meeting the women didn't get very far, and I think the point should be made pretty soon. The existence of a lesbian caucus in the New York Gay Liberation Front has been very helpful in challenging male chauvinism amongst gay men, and anti-gay feelings amongst Women's Lib.

Male Chauvinism

All men are affected by this — we are brought up that way. It means that we assume that women play subordinate roles and are less human than ourselves. At an early gay liberation meeting one guy said: 'Why don't we invite Women's Liberation — they can bring sandwiches and coffee'. It is no wonder that so few gay women have become active in our group.

Male chauvinism, however, is not central to us. We can junk it much more easily than straight men can. For we understand oppression. We have largely opted out of a system which oppresses women daily — our egos are not built on putting women down and having them build us up. Also, living in a mostly male world we have become used to playing different roles, doing our own shit-work. And finally, we have a common enemy, the big male chauvinists are also big anti-gays. But we need to purge male chauvinism, both in our behaviour and in our thoughts. Chick equals nigger equals queer. Think it over.

Women's Liberation

Women are assuming their equality and dignity and in doing so are challenging the same things we are: the roles, the exploitation of minorities by capitalism, the arrogant smugness of straight, white, pale, middle-class Britain. They are our sisters in struggle.

Problems and differences will become clear when we begin to work together. One major problem is our own male chauvinism.

Another is the uptightness and hostility to homosexuality that many women have — that is the straight in them. A third problem is differing views on sex; sex for them has meant oppression. While for us it has been a symbol of our freedom. We must come to know and understand each other's styles, jargon and humour.

Tony Reynolds

The Man I Liked Best at GLF, or The Meeting in Which We All Had To Get Into Rings

There was a man with a denim jacket there too. He also had a pipe which made him look cosy and cuddly. The tobacco smelt sweet . . . and I sat there trying to look nice but he didn't notice me. I remember him because I liked him best of all. I think he had blue eyes. Whatever he had though, he also had a nice little moustache. When we moved into rings I was disappointed because I missed him by one seat and found myself in the wrong ring. So for the moment I just sat back and tried to look nice. I agreed with points 1,2,3,4,5 and 6 [of the Principles] because I thought it would be safer to, and then turned round because I smelt the man with the moustache had lit his pipe. You could see he was a strict right-winger because he kept sticking his hand up at the wrong time. Then he looked at me and said something, but I was so busy trying to look nice for him that I missed what he said and so he turned away and said it to somebody else. The man next to him said 'Right on' and it sounded very camp. I remember because I laughed a little and looked round to see if anyone else had laughed too . . . but they hadn't, so I carried on trying to look nice and not obviously cruising. Everyone was getting very political while I was trying to look nice. I think the man who shouted 'Right on' would have said they were losing their cool. I giggled again. Then I thought I'd better do something political so I clapped and said 'Hear, hear' when the cosy man with the pipe did . . . and I said it very nicely which I thought was very nice . . . I did it a lot after that . . . I didn't seem to have a ring by then . . . I was just a sort of floating ringlet but I quite liked it because I could get on with looking nice without being disturbed too much by point 5. Then it was time to go for a drink and I lost my man with the 'no-sleeves' denim jacket and the pipe and went to get half of bitter. Someone said 'You're looking nice tonight' so I turned round and said 'Thank you', but they were't talking to me and so I was embarrassed (and nice at the same time) and asked for a light. The only trouble was I hadn't had time to roll a cigarette, so I pretended to find some matches and went to find the man with the nice smelly pipe . . . he was talking to a boy . . . I heard him say he was at the University of London. I remember thinking, how nice. I looked around to talk to someone and when I looked back he was gone, so I stopped looking nice. There was nobody else with a moustache, denim jacket (with no sleeves) and a pipe, to look nice for. It was a bit sad. I can't look nice at the GLF until next year now because I'm going home for Christmas. Maybe he'll be there next year. I'll try and look nice for him then too. I think maybe I'll take up smoking a pipe . . .

Gemini

Letter from a Brother

Dear brothers and sisters,
   I do not feel that mass meetings like dances, invasions of straight dance-halls, demonstrations, etc. should be given too much emphasis. What I think is more important to the liberation of gay people is that they mix with normal society in natural numbers, twos, threes and fours, and act in a way that is natural to them. I have danced with a boy at a straight party where we were the only two gay people, and the straights were looking at us and smiling, they accepted us. I have often been to straight restaurants with my gay friends, we have held hands and enjoyed ourselves amongst the hetero lovers, and enjoyed the same wine, candlelight and romance as they without any embarrassment or ridicule. This I feel is where our integration with society is going to begin. We are not trying to become an isolated mass community, i.e. a ghetto. We want to be normal people and so we should go to normal places in normal numbers and act like we want to act.

Trevor G. Locke

Come Together
4

[February 1971]

Danger

In his letter to *Come Together* 3, Trevor Locke advances ideas which, however well intended, can do great harm to the GLF cause and all revolutionary causes. The more so because his ideas seem so reasonable. He argues for the natural integration of gay people with 'normal society'. We are not, he says, trying to become a ghetto. We want to be normal people . . . Do we?

Do we really want to be integrated with a society we regard as sick? Do you really want to be accepted by so-called normal people? On whose terms? No. When the outside world is diseased, the ghetto is sanctuary. True, the inhabitants of the ghetto are diseased too. But the symptoms of the disease are recognisable — in the 'screaming queen', the 'leather queen', the 'skinhead queen'. The sickness being identifiable, it becomes susceptible to treatment. But the sickness of the stockbroker, banker and lawyer is hidden from the individual and society. Like syphillis, it is a sickness that is most dangerous when the symptoms are not seen.

When society grows well, the word 'normal' will cease to be meaningful.

Eric Elphenbein

Bust to Show the Flag

I was out of love that night. Well fuck it, if it's a drag I can always get pissed, or maybe even high. That was the state my head was in when I arrived at the Prince of Wales in Hampstead Road, where the GLF disco was being held on Friday 22nd January. I don't go to pubs very often, and rarely can I get into dancing, so I wasn't too keen on this idea of a disco as the only alternative scene that GLF (i.e. *we*) had managed to come up with. But it was really nice to walk into the pub and be confronted with a few friendly, familiar faces, and the offer of a drink from a guy who wasn't trying to pick me up. This was a *gay* pub for the night, but happily without the hallmarks of the gay pubs and clubs that I've been into before. Here were *people*. Happy, smiling, touching, talking, and not walking away with the impression of having talked to just 'nice-fitting pants' or 'pretty face'. Sure there were plenty of nice-fitting pants *and* pretty faces. I saw them. But I could also feel the nice vibes that came from these people. So together we danced, we talked, we touched, and we *dug it*. We were digging it . . .

KNOCK KNOCK who's there

KNOCK KNOCK who's there

ME who's that ME

oh well you'd better come in then

Evening all, we have reason to believe that there are drugs on the premises. Who's in charge?

No one's in charge. We're a group of people who've come together TOGETHER.

Alright, men over there, women over here. And they went through our pockets, and they went into our bags, and into our hair, and la la la was there anywhere they didn't look?

Well, it seemed that everyone was clean, not a nasty reefer in sight. One thing though. I and several other people who were there have been searched for drugs several times before, and they were always very much more thorough than that. I don't think that's why they were there at all, do you? They didn't even bring any lady policemen with them, so the sisters underwent an extremely tepid handbag search. But I did hear a policeman say something about 'showing the flag' — don't know what he could have been talking about, the only flag I could see was ours, we're homosexuals and proud to be so.

During the search the policemen asked some sisters and brothers for their names and addresses (among other things). They have every right to ask, but you have every right to *refuse*, and you should do so. This is just one point that all GLF members should be aware of and remember.

After the raid the police had a little chat with the landlord, intimidating him to the extent that we can no longer hold any functions at his pub. Up until this point the landlord, who was a really nice guy, had been very keen that we continue to use his pub. So we find another place. I'm sure we can see to it that it's bigger than the last and that more people will be able to get together and smile and dance and touch and *dig it*.

Power to all Oppressed People.   Paul

We Were Always Out

We were always out. We were the contorted public face of all of you and you were our good quiet uncle tom brothers.

In being queens, unmistakeably, we have always been the everyday confrontation with outside the gender role. We gave up our personal humanity for reality based on plastic: Gucci and Revlon. Our comedy was a very total refusal of control of our souls, whatever they may hide now. We died for that truth.

But you, homosexual men, and women, you are the splitting image of the Man — male and female — who puts us all down. When I hear you speak of consideration for your dear parents, I am angry. You refuse to honestly reject their controls, deny them obedience, passivity, confront their goddam decaying fantasy world. Strike your fucking parents; they and their, you and your trashy sensibility are my oppressors, and that contrived lifestyle pushes us all into a dark corner. The way-it-is is based comfortably on our every 'Yessir', our every letting the control myth pass without speaking up. Every easy lying silence is a vicious and selfish act.

If you are not part of the solution, you are part of the problem. You are an uncle tom and a pig, and you have nothing real to lose, except both our disgust at you.

You must kill the old society within your own self and your own life, or it will take you with it in its endless grey cage. You are a free agent, and slavery exists only in your head.You and only you, perpetuate our past amd make our present.

edsel

Yakkity Yak Don' Talk Back

Gay people were offered tea and sympathy on the Jimmy Saville show *Speakeasy*. It is usually a public show with an audience of 300, but because of the 'delicate nature' of the subject, the audience of fifty was both invited and exclusively homosexual. Ten sisters and brothers from GLF went along, and though we didn't like the special arrangements or the producer's attitude, we took a look at the audience and knew we had to stay.

Official speakers for the straight gay world were Humphrey Berkeley (ex-MP who proposed the bill of 1967), Michael Delanoy (Albany Trust), and Sheila, editor of *Arena Three* and — wait for it! — *Curious*!* They put the usual homosexual plea

* *Arena Three* was a lesbian journal of the time, *Curious* an 'educational' sex magazine.

for tolerance, Jimmy Saville asked the usual questions and the straight gays gave the usual answers.

'What is a homosexual? What makes a person homosexual? When did you first realise that you were homosexual? What is your favourite homosexual joke?'

Basically everyone played ball. The producer played heavy schoolmaster (I'm the boss, Jim'), Jimmy Saville played patronising social worker, the straight gays humble case histories, and GLF unruly student hippies. Jimmy Saville controlled the discussion as chairman, ignoring GLF when he could, encouraging the straight gays to enlighten 'the ignorant folk in the provinces who don't understand'; the producer fulfilled his obligation to Lord Reith and 'good radio' by cutting dull trivia such as aversion therapy (behaviourist electric shock/nausea torture), homosexuality in HM forces and government, conditioning by media and schools, homosexuals as an oppressed minority group. Fortunately there *was* time to hear about kind priests, Samaritans and social workers who might help 'the different child' to come to terms with their 'sexual problem', and the Albany Trust plan: invite your neighbour to dinner and integrate. And the lovely Lois Lane sang three memorable songs.

It was a valuable lesson in the media's control of information, and respect for the myths of bourgeois unreality.

Edsel and Richard

Murder

Sisters and brothers we are deeply concerned. We are concerned about the brutal murder of a gay man a few weeks ago on Hampstead Heath behind the Spaniards Inn. This is a well-known gay cruising ground. *Are we going to take much more of this shit,* or are we going to sit back and say, 'We all know there's a risk involved in going cruising, and besides some people are into the fear bit'?

It should be obvious that this isn't good enough, we've got to put an end to the systematic murder of gay people by sexually and socially frustrated 'queer-bashers'. If gay people are not given adequate protection by the so-called forces of 'law and order', then we must start protecting ourselves. It has been suggested that GLF self-defence karate classes be set up. All sisters and brothers who can help or who have knowledge of karate should come to GLF general meetings and offer their help.

Another suggestion has been that we start our own people's patrol force, to patrol lonely cruising grounds and to warn cruisers of the dangers. However our forces are as yet a little thin for this. Another idea is that we leaflet cruising grounds telling people about gay liberation and self-defence groups.

But whenever we see cases of brutality towards gay sisters and brothers we should go immediately to their aid. Only when gay people start to stand up for themselves will the queer-bashing lot begin to have second thoughts about their activities . . . No doubt the phenomenon of queer-bashing is a result of uncertainty over masculinity and a secret fear of their own homosexuality.

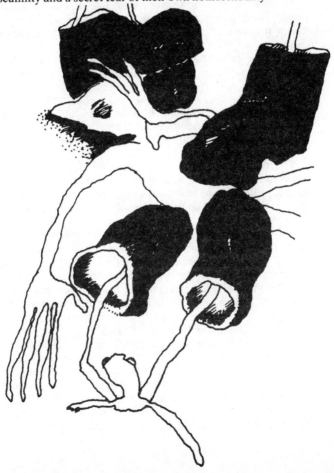

The Importance of Participation of the Base in GLF

On Saturday 16th January we had a think-in to get ourselves more together. On the whole it was a great success, though there were a few hang-ups. Everyone had the opportunity to get involved in the discussions, unlike the general meetings. The actual structure of the think-in mitigated against its domination by the experienced and over-articulate. One sad thing was that not many sisters attended.

It consisted of three sessions, each one devoted to a specific topic. The topics were: education and awareness; dealing with the media and our campaign; and organisation and premises, etc. However, we never really got round to discussing our campaign, though one thing that was heavily discussed was the role that straights should play in GLF. During each session we split into small groups, and after a set time we all came together to iron out and collate the decisions of the smaller groups. The whole thing was done in an atmosphere of friendliness and committment, though it must be admitted that there were tensions between certain more conservative members and the more radical brothers and sisters.

The think-in recommended that an education, or discovery and research group, should be set up, that central premises be found, preferably in the form of a shop-front and offices; and that groups should be set up to deal with finance, the law, and how to handle the press.

Not all of the recommendations of the think-in were well received by the following general meeting. Some people even voiced the opinion that the think-in had no right to come to decisions, but at the same time blaming the steering committee for the think-in recommendations and for not being strong enough to handle decisions themselves. It often seems that those who say the steering committee isn't strong enough, also complain about manipulation by the same.

It would seem that all these hostilities are due to two basic views of what gay liberation is all about. On the one hand are those who would like to see GLF as a strong, centrally organised, national body, complete with central executive committee, etc. formulating all the major decisions, with a full-time staff and perhaps annual election of officers, etc. On the other hand there are those of us who see GLF as having a more organic structure, where the real power and decision-making lie at the base with the small group — local, functional, or whatever, where there is no real national executive but instead a national office whose aim would be to provide the necessary coordination, services, etc. Too many come along to GLF meetings expecting that the steering committee are going to run things for them. But shit, the point of gay liberation is to get gay people to run things and their own lives themselves. For too long we've sat back and expected bishops and other notables to do things for us, we must begin to rely on our own efforts. A people's organisation like GLF must build up real base participation. Groups such as the Theatre Group, the Discovery and Research Group, the Media Workshop, the Action Group, are far more important than the steering committee. Many people blame the steering committee for not running the general meetings in a better manner, but the responsibility for the general meeting does not lie with them but with you and me as individual members of GLF. Too often the general meetings are the scenes of individual ego-trips which, however articulate, are geared not to making sure the meeting works, only to making sure that the individual has his say.

That's why the think-in was such a refreshing contrast. All superstars or potential superstars should be put down and highly criticised because they limit the possibilities of GLF and intimidate the less articulate. Ego-tripping is part and parcel of our oppressive society and must be overcome. No one person should carry more weight than any other, no matter how much 'experience' they've had.

One way of dealing with the problem of ego-tripping is the setting up of awareness groups. This was recommended on a trial basis by the think-in, but met with heavy opposition from many people at the general meeting. They said that we weren't ready for them and that we were ignorant of the methods. Mao says, 'Dare to struggle, dare to win', and we should follow this maxim. So what if we are ignorant of the correct methods, we must learn by our own mistakes and successes. If we have a real committment, then we will succeed despite the warnings of the 'better informed'.

Aubrey

Come Together

GLF Against the IRB

The Gay Liberation Front showed en masse on Sunday 21st February, in a vast demonstration, that oppression by the Big State Machine also affects gay people and that they are as interested in fighting it as are all other groups that suffer from it. For this reason we were there when the TUC demonstrated against the Industrial Relations Bill — the government's big dictatorial measure to stop working people fighting for their rights.

We were not only there because as a liberation front we aim to help fight all forms of oppression, but also because many, in fact most, of the people on the demo were real male chauvinists themselves, and therefore our enemy. We were there to *confront* the male chauvinism of working people. We felt that if we could get people to let go of their male privilege they will have no further interest in this oppressive system, and will therefore fight harder against it.

So our presence was really important, because we are starting to work alongside women, black people, and now those sections of youth and the working class who see the importance of *our* demands as well as their own, to break the old society which puts us all down and to build a new one on the basis of all our needs.

Bill

Hey Man

Every man growing up in this culture is programmed to systematically oppress, dehumanise, objectify and rape women. A man's cock, a biological accident, becomes the modus operandi by which a male child is bestowed with power by this culture. A mere couple of inches of flesh places this male child in a position above half the human race, and there is no man who does not benefit and glorify in the power inherent in this birthright. Every expression of manhood is a reassertion of this cock privilege. All men are male supremacists. Gay men are no exception to the maxim.

The ability to express homosexuality, however, carries with it a severe penalty in our culture, because of the nature of the taboo placed upon homosexuality by this male-dominated heterosexual society. Straight men abhor homosexuality because of their inability and inadequacy when it comes to expressing love for another man. Heterosexual men are driven to abuse women because they can't directly express the love they have for each other. They literally fuck their friends' women because they are unable to fuck their friends.

Homosexuality is a manifestation of the breaking down of male roles. This 'unacceptable' affront to conventional manhood forces male straight society up against the wall; so much so that they must suppress, repress and oppress all signs of a life-giving homosexuality and force it into their warped, death-dealing definitions. Their task, then, becomes a bludgeoning of homosexuality into a heterosexual parodistic expression within this culture. Gay men are violently driven toward a false goal: the mutation of homosexuality into a male heterosexual persona. This results in the constant struggle of gay men to fit themselves into a heterosexual ideation of manhood. The gay man is asked to love, emulate and worship his oppressor. The oppression gay men suffer has shown the validity and absolute necessity for a struggle for gay liberation. We have begun in our struggle for liberation to reject the internalisation of this male heterosexual identity. Gay men must examine all forms of their homosexuality and be suspicious of all of them, because the ways we express homosexuality have been moulded by male supremacy. The gay liberation struggle will not reach beyond the civil libertarian goals of the homophile movement until it can see how deeply ingrained and oppressive is this idealisation of male heterosexuality within each of us.

Gay Liberation Front men have avoided the question of male supremacy, as if they were exempt. *Indeed, it is the most crucial question relevant to any struggle for gay liberation.* Male homosexuality could be the first attempt at the non-assertion of cultural manhood. It could be the beginning of the process by which we can reach a gender redefinition of Man: the 'non-man'. Homosexuality from this standpoint is the first step in the process of 'de-manning'. The men of GLF have instead consistently asserted their manhood, resulting in an attempt to stifle the struggle of women to free themselves from the shackles of male domination. What is worse is that GLF men have further used the presence of women to legitimise their homosexuality. An examination of GLF results in the conclusion that the gay men are no less afraid of each other than are straight men without 'their women'. What is pervasive in GLF is a resistance to examining our sexual repression, inhibition, and puritanism. If sexuality is expressed, it is done behind closed doors. GLF men have dutifully continued to use The Man's exploitative institutions, which are designed to keep us in our oppression. To be blunt, we have accepted The Man's roles and go to him to get laid.

Gay Liberation Front men have either avoided or attacked the most important movement in the world today: the struggle for the liberation of women. Any organisation which does not recognise this struggle is objectively counter-revolutionary. We have fought male supremacy in every one of our relationships with men. We should know what women are talking about. In order to join the struggle for women's liberation, we as gay men must relinquish all power in GLF to the women. We must give them final veto power. Until GLF men join the struggle, we will either drive the women out or continue to subvert them, thus becoming the young, hip, counterculture version of the Mattachine Society. It is in the interests, however, of GLF to join this struggle. Combatting male supremacy, in ourselves and in other men, is in fact at the very heart — or should be — of our struggle against our oppression.

The commitment needed for a struggle for liberation carries with it heavy demands. We must begin to make demands on each male GLF member. GLF must demand the complete negation of the use of gay bars, tearooms, trucks, baths, streets, and other traditional cruising institutions. These are exploitative institutions designed to keep gay men in the roles given to them by a male heterosexual system. The use of these institutions by GLF men must be seen as copping out to The Man's oppression of homosexuals. We will instead begin to remould our homosexuality by developing a communistic sexuality of sharing, cooperation, selflessness, and total community. Our commitment to fight for gay liberation will be the means by which we can devise the necessary tactics for the destruction of all exploitative gay institutions and of all male-supremacist institutions. Our recognition of male heterosexuality as our oppressor will mean that we have to confront every male heterosexual with whom we come into contact.

We have been kept in isolation, we have been oppressed, exploited, and our identity has been taken from us. We have been told how to be gay and where to go to express it. It is no accident that we have been forced into the Gay Liberation Front to fight. Our homosexuality can be a revolutionary tool only if we abandon our self-destructive attempts to fit the warped roles given us by the male heterosexual system. The fear that one might be thought homosexual by another man — this fear is a powerful goad keeping men, both homosexual and heterosexual, in line as the oppressors of women. It is one of the many ways that men hold on to their privileges derived from oppression. Our task lies before us: our goal is stopping the propagation of the male heterosexual ethos by any means necessary.

We are backed to the wall. There is no turning back. Our rage will no longer eat at our bowels. We have seen who has done it. We can feel him; identify him. My 'brothers' in the movement, they pleaded: 'Don't be divisive. Work with me for the revolution.' But it is a revolution born of their discontent: it is a Man revolution. The Man revolution with women to fuck, bear their children, lick their wounds and cook their meals. Faggots to be put away. They are the same men who put me behind barbed wire in Cuba. They watched me peek out at what I had fought alongside of them for; what I had died with them for. They are the same white supremacists who told blacks they had gone too far. They didn't give up their white-skin privileges. Instead they waited for blacks to come home. But blacks didn't come home to Mastah Man and neither will women. Men of the movement, we know you are Amerika. You are not revolutionaries, but the capitalist ideal of rugged individualism. Women and gay people will stop your revolution; it is male counter-revolution.

I don't want your help, understanding, or sympathy. I can recognise that, your male-supremacist jive. Your love is oppression; it means bondage. I will fight the capitalists, that is inevitable. Capitalism is another word for male supremacy. You,

movement heterosexual man — Man, you are the ruling class.
Hey Man, are you fighting to keep your inherited power? Listen
Man, give it up or go under. Your universe is being smashed.
Your fantasy is being challenged. My soul won't be cast-ironed
out by your drunken raps. A timing of barricades will come: on
which side will you be?

Steve Dansky

Silver Surfer Versus Imperial College Man

After a lot of talk it was decided to do it in straight drag. The prospect was frightening as no one had done drag before in their lives and we wanted to get away from the drag image. But we eventually agreed that it was essential if we were to aim at confusing the sexual roles in the minds of these students, in the all-male bar at Imperial College.

The attack was double-edged. The men and one brave girl in drag went ahead to infiltrate, followed ten minutes later by Women's Lib and our Street Theatre group — the girls dressed as men and some of the men dressed as women — beautifully made-up and dressed to kill. By accident one woman from Women's Lib got mixed up with the advance party and on arrival was jeered by the students in the bar who gave orders to the barman to 'do his stuff'. This freaked the GLF men who gathered protectively around Sue, dressed as a man, but who nevertheless got it together, leaned on the bar and ordered a pint which the unsuspecting bar stooge served. By this time the 'ladies' arrived, and ignoring the jeering and shouts that greeted us from the students, met up with their 'boyfriends' and tried to get a drink. We were refused, and so we grouped ourselves in the centre of the room, split these gross, pint-sinking 15-stone heavies into two factions, and decided to ask them why they were so frightened of women. Advance parties tripped out from our central cluster to ask, but were defeated by answers a seven-year-old schoolkid could have bettered. But we made our point and touched these juvenile Powellites on some very soft spot. The reaction was startling, as they then realised that some of the women were men, then, very slowly, they hit on it — the men were homosexuals.

They stumbled about in a daze, they were nearly outnumbered, the only thing they could do was phone for supporters. Meanwhile, so as not to lose control it was suggested that our sisters dressed as men and the sisters from Women's Lib should kiss these beery brutes, but this beautiful gesture was turned down with the now common chant that they preferred wanking. So leaving them in their corners, we turned and kissed each other. There we were, men kissing men, women kissing women, every combination you could think of, right in the middle of this bar at Imperial College. Shouts and antagonism rose on either side, you could sense the ones behind you mentally creeping up and hitting you. We tensed, and kissed, and waited, fear creeping up our backs, but nothing happened. We turned, and they were rooted, hypnotised, and while it lasted, physically passive. Then, true to the age of their mental arrest they whooped into the lavatory and returned to fight us with a hosepipe. Not expecting water cannons, we made for the door.

Then someone shouted: 'It's only water, girls, come on and enjoy it', and we did. The place was wrecked, water everywhere as we stood, silent and defiant, until they advanced with baseball bats and physically threw us out and locked the door. We stood in the door, make-up running, mascara stories becoming true, freezing cold, wet and very angry. We were gay, we were GLF, and as their smutty rugby songs seeped through the door from the bar we drowned them with shouting: 'Give us a "G", give us an "A", give us a "Y", what does that spell? GAY'.

Then, gathering ourselves together, we marched to the mixed bar for a well-earned drink, and to explain to any students who cared to listen what had happened. For some of us it was the first time we'd rapped to straights about Gay Lib, and although they didn't agree with everything we said they were very sympathetic, not only to us, but to what had happened in the other bar. Finally we sat talking and relaxing together when suddenly we found ourselves surrounded by the pigs from the other bar. They had worked themselves up in their war-dance of rugby songs, and red-faced and sweating they were out for blood. Some of the students we had been talking to tried to intervene, but the pigs turned round and pushed them up to the bar. We were then grabbed and shoved to the foot of the stairs leading to the street, and then repeatedly charging heads down they threw us out onto the pavement. They stood and jeered, we stood and argued. Unnoticed by us, the steady escalation of agro and aggression really helped us to get it on, and cool accurate insults came roaring out of our heads, even when more water was showered down from the building above and a crowd began to gather on the opposite pavement. Eventually the fascist pigs retired inside, and just as the fuzz arrived, we leapt into a taxi and headed home. The Phantom Fairies had struck, left havoc behind them, and disappeared into the night, leaving nothing but a faint smell of perfume on the air. All of us thought that students were real cool, until we went to Imperial College.

A Queen Really is a Person

First, I must say, I am a queen — perhaps one of the campest variety. Since joining GLF three months ago I have been asking myself 'Why?', and am I happy with myself? I ask the first question because I see so many other gay boys at the general meetings who, although obviously feminine, are not queens. At last, I think I've got the answer. First of all, when I was launched into the Gay World proper, I was conditioned by Gay Society into being camp — it was the thing to be. All my friends had gone through the same process, so I followed suit, older people found us amusing.

I soon realised that I wanted to 'come out', but found it extremely difficult, as do all gay people when they are very young. So I finally left home on my seventeenth birthday and came to the big metropolis. Here I found people didn't care as much as in Bournemouth, so my 'coming out' was quite automatic. But in this, the conditioning by the Gay World continued, so I became more camp, and the more people I found liked me, the more camp I got! Where will it all end, you may ask yourself — where indeed? To me, coming out was simply to camp oneself in front of straights. It was all good clean fun, and I had many good times. But then my second boyfriend left me, and in doing so told me I was far too camp. This was a shock to me, because I thought that was what one was suppposed to be. No, they all said. Don't take any notice of them, all the queens said, they're only men, and what do they know? And so, there lies sexism in the Gay World. Sad, isn't it? I was one of its victims, and if it were possible to do so, I would regret it. But there we are.

'Am I happy?' Well, I've decided not. Life shouldn't be one long ego-trip, and a daily performance, seven days a week, fifty-two weeks a year, gets so boring, for everyone. What can I do? This is hard to answer. Just don't camp, be yourself, the men (whoops, there I go again) might say. I often start the day off alright, but then something happens and off I go again, screaming my tits off.

I am very politically minded and very 'aware', so I enjoy the lively GLF meetings, and get quite excited when someone stands up, red faced, and shouts back at someone else. Then someone says something about a lot of screaming queens — *bang*, that hurt. I tell myself queens have a part to play in GLF, and society at large, and all my friends agree. So what am I really worried about? Can anyone tell me?

Richard Shipp

Straight?

One of the questions that has troubled many people almost since the beginning of GLF is whether or not to allow straight people to participate in the organisation. This problem was hotly debated at the think-in last January, but its recommendation that straight people should not be allowed to vote at meetings, or to serve on committees, met with opposition from several sisters and brothers at the following weekly meeting and was finally voted against. However, the question was again raised more recently at the last elections to the steering committee, and is still in many people's minds.

It is puzzling to many gay people why heterosexuals should want to play a part in what is essentially a homosexual organisation. Do they come out of a spirit of curiosity, to see what homosexuals are like, so that GLF becomes a peep-show for prurient straights? Is it because they find gay people 'so sweet', and come for a patronising reason? Is it because they are secretly or unconsciously gay themselves but haven't yet dared admit it? Or do they come because Gay Liberation is this year's trendy organisation? I do not mean to put straight people down; I am merely putting forward some of the questions that have been asked by many of our gay sisters and brothers during recent months. It would be interesting to know the answers.

Any suggestion that straight people should not be allowed to join GLF immediately receives the accusation of being sexist. Surely, it is argued, if Gay Lib demands the end of sexual discrimination and the abolition of sex labelling, then it would be against our principles to ban heterosexuals from our meetings and even to take any account of their sexual orientation at all. If they are prepared to support GLF and work for it, we should make them welcome.

Contrary to this it can be argued that gay people have let straights run things for them for too long, and that now is the time for gay people to stand on their own feet and organise themselves together *by themselves*, without any help (however well meant) from straight people. Straight people have been our oppressors for so long that it seems paradoxical to have them telling us how to run our organisation. It is time for homosexuals to struggle to liberate themselves without relying on straights to do it for them. If we want liberation we want it on our terms without any chance of only getting it on theirs, however much they may support us. No matter how great their understanding of homosexual oppression, it is impossible for heterosexuals to identify with gay people precisely because they are not homosexual themselves. In just the same way it is impossible for me as a white man to identify with the oppressed black — I can only try to sympathise and understand his oppression; I cannot *feel* it because I am not black myself.

This does not mean that I do not recognise the worth of the part that heterosexuals have played and can play in GLF. I fully realise that our straight sisters and brothers have done a lot for Gay Liberation by helping with organisation, and I do not personally think of them as being untrustworthy. But I would rather see homosexuals in their place. Perhaps this is the fault not of the straight people who do things but rather of the gay people who come along to our meetings yet are not participating as much as they could be. Perhaps the onus is on gay people to play a much more active role, so that we should not need the talents of straight people, but could be much more of a homosexual liberation front than we are at the moment.

Gateways Bust

On Saturday, 20th February, about a hundred GLF sisters and brothers gathered at Sloane Square tube station in order to leaflet the King's Road, and ultimately to demonstrate at the Gateways Club against the barring of several women from the club for their activities in GLF. While the brothers passed down King's Road distributing leaflets, the sisters (whom I was with) went on ahead to the club in order to talk with members and hand out leaflets. Inside the club the sisters split into twos and threes to approach and talk with the women. After about thirty minutes of quiet conversations within the club, one of the sisters was dragged to the foot of the stairs where Gina (the owner) pulled her up several steps by the hair. Pandemonium did not break loose. One of the sisters pulled the plug out of the juke-box and shouted 'Gay is Good!', while the rest of the sisters, who had already finished distributing leaflets to the women in the club, quietly filed out of the doors to join the brothers outside.

We had not been out of the club for more than five minutes when the police arrived to tell us to break up and move along. Walking along King's Road in couples and groups of three, one of the sisters who had stopped and was standing quietly at the end of the bus queue outside the Antique Market was arrested for 'obstructing the free passage of the footpath', and was pulled away by the arm by a policeman. A number of sisters and brothers climbed into the police van voluntarily, so that the sister would not go alone to the station, while other GLF sisters and brothers were dragged and shoved into the van by the police.

At the station we found that the police had arrested thirteen of us in all, plus two young boys who were standing at the bus stop waiting for a bus — they had never even heard of GLF. The boys pleaded guilty to the charge of 'obstructing the free passage of the highway' and were given £1 fines. Marshall, an American brother who was arrested with us, and whose visa had expired, was given 'supervised passage' home and is now active in New York GLF. Lala and I, who came up in court the 5th of this month [March], were fined £3 each plus an additional £5 to cover court costs, in spite of four witnesses whose testimony plainly contradicted that of the single police constable testifying against us. The rest of the sisters and brothers will come up for trial later this month.

Carla

Come Together
6

Male/Female

As a gay sister of GLF I intended to write an article on gay sexuality, but in writing I found no way of avoiding the extent to which female sexuality has been influenced by social role concepts. We are all channelled from the moment of birth into roles determined by the genitals we happen to possess. From that moment onwards we are thrust into specific roles divided from each other — divided from ourselves. We are either male or female — one half or the other half.

As human beings we instinctively possess the same qualities, but have learnt to regard aggression, assertion, dominance as male qualities, and passivity, emotionality and sensitivity as female qualities. We have exploited these factors of ourselves according to our gender and have repressed those which are assumed to be appropriate to the opposite sex. Men are conditioned to stifle emotions and are not allowed the energy release of crying. Women are not expected to voice opinions or assert themselves in the presence of men. In actuality we are only exploring 50 per cent of our being; the other 50 per cent is buried somewhere.

The female is the most violated in the role enactment, largely because society is based on the family nucleus — the male, the female, and their produce. Physiologically women in a family unit eventually become child-bearing, house-bound placators of the male ego. Sexuality becomes a playground for the enactment of our male/female games. The straight male's concept of sexuality is clearly embodied in his sexual terminology of fucking, laying and screwing, in which the woman's role is to be fucked, layed and screwed, and to dig it. It is unfortunate that the 'submissive and receptive' female rarely fucks, lays or screws 'her man'.

Women have largely accepted this passive role, and have been made to fear their own sexuality. It is not expected of woman to take an active role in the sexual act — her body is used to being prone, her body is used to being fucked. If she is stricken with fear and anguish at the act of violence perpetrated against her body, then she is frigid and of no consequence. If she has an awareness of her sexual needs and desires she is termed a 'loose woman' or a 'good lay' or a whore. In fact, women are so sexually oppressed by men that it is not acknowledged that her sexual energies are equal to those of the men. In actual fact her sexual energies are quite often more resilient; as the beautiful Martha Shelley (Radical Lesbians, New York) said, 'We can keep it going longer'.

Consider the motivation in male/female sexuality. By total lifestyles engendered upon us the male is the dominant, the female the submissive. I believe we have not successfully rid ourselves of our instincts; the act of sexuality for men is one of guilt. Guilt breeds through his endeavours to repress the fear and contempt he feels to his own femininity. It is a threat to his identity as a male, a challenge to his masculine ego, to acknowledge a duality.

The woman is the epitome of those things he cannot allow himself to be. Sexuality for him is thus an act of alienation. He is in himself loathing fucking that part of himself that he cannot accept. Sexual action between an oppressor and his oppressed is an act of violence not of love.

Since becoming gay I have gone through a process of relearning and discovery, as I know have many other of the sisters. It has meant becoming aware of oppression, of role-playing, of head-fucking. Of becoming aware of sensuality as opposed to sexuality, of the body as opposed to the genitals. Of becoming aware of a being instead of a half being.

All Power to Our Sisters and Brothers.

Barbara

Building the Alternative Gay Collectives

As a gay person I have lived within myself all my life. I have torn myself apart, destroyed and hidden myself, even from myself. I tried to become butcher than butch, fucking as many women as possible to prove that I was a Man. But my gayness still broke through. I avoided 'male sports', preferring rounders and netball, if anything at all. I grew my hair in direct response to my mother's complaints about effeminacy, stole my sister's panties to wear and cruised at every available opportunity. Even so I put down 'queers' whenever the subject arose — I was the uptightest, straightest closet queen you had ever seen.

So where does this 'confession' lead? It leads to the rationale behind this article, a rationale which, I feel, that if GLF people follow will lead to a higher level of consciousness and a general tightening up of political direction to replace the low-level floundering that presently characterises GLF.

The rationale is that of collective living, that of a group of people living and working together, consciously trying to attack the perverted ways in which we were brought up and struggling together to find a new way of living and relating to people. It is this rationale which brought me out, which stopped me regarding women and men as hunks of meat or sex objects, and is teaching me to regard myself, and others, as people and not a set of attitudes or various fucked-up definitions imposed by outside society.

One of the major purposes of GLF is to redefine our attitudes and lifestyles to understand how we, as people, have been exploited and oppressed because of our love for each other, and to fight back against that exploitation and oppression. Thus we must work out the most positive way in which we can begin to fight back. Most of us attend the weekly GLF meeting, and perhaps one other group meeting, and then go back to the bedsit in Earl's Court or to the flat we share with one or two friends.

'For an oppressed group to successfully challenge those who control them they have to be able to create, construct a total alternative kind of being. Such an alternative does not drop from the skies. It has to be hewn out through suffering, in struggle, over time, and with thought.'(Sheila Rowbotham, *Women's Liberation and The New Politics*.)

It is only through consciously struggling with a group of people that this alternative being can develop, and that cannot be done in the context of a bedsit or that of a few friends casually sharing a flat together. The most effective way to transform our lives in toto (a very frightening prospect at first), I feel is to live collectively, in groups of between five and eight, where criticism and self-criticism become positive tools in the struggle, where the love and support from the rest of the collective help each individual in their struggle to clear out the shit inside their heads, planted by more than 2,000 years of Judeo-Christian heterosexual male-supremacist ethic. It is a struggle we can only begin, but it is an immensely rewarding struggle, where the results of the changes inside our heads and in our lifestyles prove that the pain of being honest and accepting criticism and changing because of it are worthwhile.

We must remember that one of the greatest weapons we have against those who control our lives is that 'our strength grows out of the rightness of our causes and the trust we have of each other. By moving and working in small groups before the repressive forces we learn to trust each other more and threaten more effectively the powers over our lives'. (Agitprop Collective, *The Bust Book*.)

Let's use that weapon, let's use it to smash the system which has oppressed us and distorted us into mimicking the Man's society. We've talked about the alternative society for long enough, it's about time we started to create it.

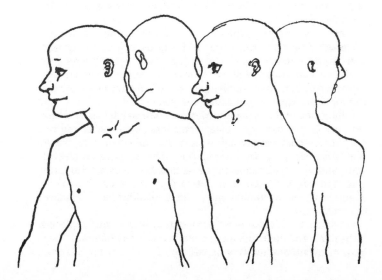

Male Gay Roles

Leather queens; skinhead queens; muscle queens; chicken queens; race queens; dress queens; head queens; cottage queens...

Searching for fulfilment of their adolescent sex fantasy (their 'type'). Engaging in the 'hunt'. Cruising each other. Playing 'games' with each other. Games of destruction. Prick teasing.

Looking, obsessively and furtively, not for love or friendship or brotherhood, but for the other actor to assert his gay 'role' with. To stage the same *one-act* play with, then disappear, tossing the phone number into the gutter, in his guilt and shame. Guilt at being homosexual, shame at being unable to be proud of his sexuality.

Hiding and role-playing; acting and pretending; leading the double life and denying his homosexuality. Playing the straight male role society has imposed on him in his daily life, it extends into his 'gay' night life.

I am not me! I am Danny La Rue, Barbra Streisand, Marlene Dietrich, Bardot, Moreau, Marlon Brando, James Dean, Steve Reeves, Mick Jagger, Joe Dalessandro.

Playing the same continuous role, trapped for life, drained of any individual personality, he loses himself in the part. He buries what he knows to be the real him — lonely and afraid. Lonely because he's afraid of love and friendship. He has lost his self-confidence.

Afraid to examine himself, he does not even know or understand himself. And afraid of being discovered by straight society, he becomes afraid of being 'discovered' by his gay brothers, and afraid to discover them — lest the erotic fantasy turns out to be a man, fallible, erratic, often happy, sometimes sad, but needing love and understanding.

Playing roles in a society which demands gender definitions, sexual role-playing, masculine versus feminine — what can we do, those whom society dismisses and condemns as half-men? Too often we react by over-playing. The absurd parodies of straight sexuality we see in the bars, ultra-butch, camp bitch, are cold and brittle. Their eyes betray fear and loathing as they compete viciously, to allay the panic of loneliness at the end of the night.

As time passes, tenderness, sensitivity are frozen out, replaced by hysteria and neuroticism, and utter conformity of mind. They become aware that they are outcasts.

For men like these — men like us — liberation is around the corner. GLF will fight and destroy this obscene oppression. Be free. Be yourself.

The cottage is the coffin — come out and live! Meet our brothers and sisters. They are homosexual and they are beautiful! And they are happy, and they are angry; because they are proud and love one another.

The meat-market smells! Drink up and leave the racketeering bars! Pull the flush in the cottage! Have a revolution in your life!

Two Letters

Dearest Gay Liberation Front,

I love you. I think you are wonderful. I am one of your kind but, sorry to say, my position at work, the fact that I have a wife and two kids, prevents me from joining your meetings. In other words, I can't declare my homosexuality. My parents, friends and family would probably cut me off completely. However this is what you are trying to change and I am glad. Long life to you.

You may ask, if I am married how can I be gay? But I am. I rarely make love to my wife now. We have talked about this and I know that she goes with other men; some of them I know. She thinks that I go out with other girls but actually I do not. For some time, about two months, I was meeting a youth every Friday and we would go out in my car. Sometimes I chance upon a gay person in toilets or swimming pools. I once met a gay boy when I went pony-trekking and we had sex even though it was risky.

I really see nothing wrong with homosexuals and do not think it is disgusting or morally wicked. I wish everyone thought as I do. Please do not mind me not signing this letter. I am only twenty-six and if people found out, my whole life would be ruined.

Wishing you all power and freedom to love as we choose,

Yours,

XXX

Dear brother,

Thanks for your letter. We are sorry that you feel unable to come out into the open about being gay. There are many people in similar positions to you who find it very difficult to be themselves in the situations that they have gotten into. And of course because so many keep their true feelings hidden, the nature and extent of homosexuality remains unrealised by the rest of society.

It is only by coming out, and coming out proud, that we can ever be truly liberated. Not only does it confront straight people with our existence, but it also liberates ourselves from the tensions, guilt and hypocrisy of pretence.

You say you are married. That doesn't surprise us — there are a number of married people in GLF who have managed to declare their homosexuality and have gained a great sense of relief from at last being open and having nothing to hide. What is more important — yourself or your family and friends? If they can't accept the real you, and you'll probably find that they can, then are they worth worrying about? GLF provides an opportunity for you to meet other people who will accept you as you are and enable you to build up new, more rewarding friendships.

We fully realise the pressures on you, but while you succumb to these pressures you will never be able to attain full happiness. The choice is yours. Either remain in your present unhappy state or else build a new lifestyle. If you choose the latter, GLF can help you. Why not come along to one of our meetings and find out what Gay Liberation means?

Come Together (Women's Issue) 7

[*July 1971*]

Introduction

We share the experiences of our gay brothers but as women we have endured them differently. Whereas the men in GLF partake of the privileges of the male — you have been allowed to organise, talk and dominate — we have been taught not to believe in ourselves, in our judgement, but to act dumb and wait for a man to make the decisions. As lesbians, 'women without men', we have always been the lowest of the low. Only through acting collectively can we overcome our own passivity and your male chauvinism so that together we — the whole of GLF — can smash the sexist society which perverts and imprisons us all.

WE'RE WOMEN
WE'RE LESBIANS
WE'RE OPPRESSED
WE'RE ANGRY

Where It's At

Up till now gay-ins have always been West End occasions in parks situated in affluent areas — beautiful houses and well-dressed people with nicely washed children. Yes, it was all very pleasing to the eye: the world was beautiful and we, the GLF, were busy liberating ourselves and the gay people of the West End. I am sure it is a good thing to stimulate other gay people to come out and thus to strengthen their belief in themselves.

I am also sure that GLF is not just an organisation which aims at making homosexuals happier through their 'acceptance' of their specific sexual preference. *We are a front.* Which should mean a militant organisation, a growing group of people who can identify with other oppressed groups since our oppression springs from the same source: the capitalist state's economic necessity to exploit groups of people and its needs for scapegoats (since the mass of people need to do more than just watch football to work off their aggression). In this way attention is not only shifted away from the main issues, but also oppressed groups are played off against each other while the money-grabbers at the top continue their moonlight garden parties. These are basically the people and the principles we have to attack. And I mean attack, in all kinds of ways: scruples are ridiculous in situations like this. It is about time we started calling them criminals instead of capitalists. There is no use pleading with criminals, especially when they have professional protectors (the police) and a publicity machine (the media).

To attack all this GLF must be militant and tough. And this brings me back to the gay-ins. As I see it, West End gay-ins can only be a preliminary stage in GLF's development. What we have been doing so far has been nothing but harvesting some fruits which were going to fall anyway. Now we must go to the East End and the poorer areas of London, firstly to talk to people and convince them that we are fighting the same people who deny them decent housing, milk for their children at school, a share in the factory's wealth, etc., and secondly to encourage East End homosexuals to come out. They are the really oppressed ones, because they have no opportunity — as richer gay people have — to lead a double life. Their workmates are their friends. And it is a working-class social necessity to act out to the full the stereotype sex roles — the male, hefty and virile; the female incomplete without the male. If they do not adhere to these roles they are bound to be rejected. So everything is bubbling under the surface. Fear and insecurity stops the crater from erupting. We need them — their anger — because we need more drive and militancy in GLF.

The Straight Gay World of Holloway

As a lesbian, I found it quite liberating to be imprisoned in Holloway. For here on some wings it was, if not actually 'queer' to be 'normal', then at least perfectly 'normal' to be 'queer'.

It was in many ways a refreshing change from the straight world outside. For the first time I found it acceptable, indeed advantageous, to be homosexual. As soon as fellow-prisoners realised you were a lesbian, you were likely to be popular and sought after — that is, if you appeared to be butch. This unwonted popularity could in fact occasionally prove something of an embarrassment! You could not strike up a platonic friendship with anyone without it being construed as an affair.

Attitudes to lesbianism varied somewhat from wing to wing. It was the accepted way of life on the wing where I spent my last sentence — an open, 'therapeutic' wing for relatively long-term old lags. Here the screws usually turned a blind eye to what went on. Couples made no attempt to hide their feelings for each other, but openly embraced and walked about arm in arm. Women could, if they wished, spend a fair amount of time alone together in pairs (or more) in their cells, with the doors pulled to. It was unwise to march straight into someone else's cell if the door was not open — most people were tactful enough to knock first.

I remember an incident in which two women were caught 'having it off' together one Saturday afternoon, when, according to the rules, they should have been either in the television room or locked up singly in their own cells. They were punished — but for breaking this minor rule, not for making love.

This quite permissive attitude on the part of the authorities was probably due to the fact that a number of them were undoubtedly lesbians themselves — as residential staff at most single-sex establishments frequently are. Some lesbian prisoners were apt to boast that actual screws had propositioned them, even offered them bribes for their favours. This may or may not occasionally have been true. The prison rules do not in fact mention homosexuality as such, but merely forbid 'indecent behaviour'.

Lesbian relationships were the norm also on the 'Borstal Recall' wing. I worked in the garden with many of the inmates of this block. They openly discussed among themselves and with their officer all that went on. But on the 'Star' wing for first offenders (where, albeit a recidivist, I once spent most of six months because I was a 'civil' prisoner), official attitudes were somewhat different — perhaps because the women here were considered redeemable and as yet uncorrupted. Here, cell doors could not be pulled to, and no less than three women at a time were supposed to be in a cell. Among the prisoners themselves on this wing, attitudes towards homosexuality were, on the whole, not quite so casually accepting as elsewhere in the prison.

Despite this openness about and acceptance of lesbian relationships on the recidivists' wing, I was amused on one occasion by the general reticence at one of the large 'group counselling' sessions. A girl was in trouble over having escaped from the wing one evening and got onto another wing where her girlfriend was living. For some time the group discussed this incident purely in terms of the ethics of the girl having got the screw in charge into trouble by managing to escape. No one seemed able to bring themselves to mention the crucial matter: the lesbian relationship. This may have been because on this particular occasion the whole wing was assembled together, plus the wing governor. Eventually I stated that we were really discussing the rights and wrongs of homosexuality. Afterwards, one or two people marvelled at my temerity.

There was a considerable amount of artificiality about Holloway lesbianism. Some of it smacked of false, schoolgirl-like 'pashes' (not that all schoolgirl pashes are false, of course) — a way, probably, of relieving the tedium of prison life. People would break rules by writing notes to each other, sometimes even when they were on the same wing, able to meet and talk openly anyway. And it was not unusual for a woman to 'turn', or pretend to have 'turned', simply because she was in Holloway, where being butch could be quite rewarding: your girlfriend was apt to keep you in fags, people chased you with offers of small gifts bought with their meagre earnings. Even accepting that most people are more or less bisexual, still it seemed reasonable to conclude that many of the Holloway butch-chasers were simply women who outside were quite straight (often mothers with families — as indeed some of the butch types themselves were), but, while inside, were merely trying to make the best of a bad job and find themselves a mock cock.

This led on to another kind of artificiality; many Holloway lesbians were appallingly straight. Whether transvestite, partially transvestite or not, it was customary for the butch types to attempt to appear in every way as masculine as possible, strapping back their busts, contriving false penises with sanitary towels, only (if what they said was true) making love — never receiving it. All this was more difficult in years gone by, when you could not wear your own clothes in Holloway. The only hope then for a butch to appear totally masculine was for her to get one of the prison jobs (gardening or painting) that entailed wearing shirt and dungarees. Otherwise, she had to do the best she could in her regulation cotton frock — roll up her cardigan sleeves to expose tattooed forearms, roll her stockings down to look like knee-socks (this was actually against the rules), cultivate pseudo-sideburns to embellish her Eton crop. Now, however, it is possible for the undiscerning visitor to Holloway to wonder whether she has made a mistake and is actually in the Scrubs. For women prisoners can wear their own clothes these days, including, if they wish, masculine gear. So butch types (phoney and genuine) can wear drag (bar belts and ties) and really go around looking like straight husbands; on open wings their femme partners may even offer to do their washing and ironing for them.

The problem now for butch and transsexual lesbians is that to appear both 'with it' and male, you should not have close cropped hair. Yet the moment the most masculine-looking female face is framed in longish hair, it inevitably ceases to look quite so male. A very butch, more or less transvestite woman on my wing started to conform with fashion and let her hair grow down her neck. At once she looked somewhat more feminine. Foolishly I suggested she cut her hair short again. She was unable however to accept that anything could ever make her remotely resemble her own sex — I merely got punched for my advice.

There is no doubt that gay women can have a sense of freedom in Holloway that, as yet, they can seldom or never experience outside. On the other hand, homosexual roles there tended to be rigid and conventional, conducive to the male chauvinism that Women's Lib and Gay Lib so firmly oppose.

Pat Arrowsmith

Revolution in the Head...

Revolution in the second part of the twentieth century is not an action. Revolution today is a *state of mind* that manifests itself through its bearer's way of acting.

Revolution isn't something that happens on the 4th or 14th of July or in February or a specific year — where it is real, it happens every minute of the day, and it starts every morning over and over again! This state of mind does not express itself particularly in so-called 'revolutionary actions' such as demonstrations, etc. It can be seen in every movement, it speaks through every word and commands every gesture of the 'revolutionary'.

As Western culture grows more and more chilly, more and more specific, i.e. as every man gradually tends to refer himself only to himself (national identity, creed identity, even family identity fade away into thin, abstract concepts), revolution changes from a time-limited incidence in one's life to a continuous *way of living*. Every man has to start with himself, with his own everyday life, and can no longer pin his hope on prophets or saints or leaders or masters or gurus or anybody else for his salvation.

Thus the idea of revolution becomes something concrete and gives freedom a possibility to enter the realm of reality.

The seed of freedom sleeps in every contemporary human being, but it does not grow out of its own nature — it has to be planted in a conscience. If consciousness does not throw light and water and warmth on this seed, it is bound to die. And so within most people the seed of freedom is killed by absent-minded survival — by things, careers, time-passing amusements or freaky, trendy, 'spontaneous' conformity.

Within people who in one way or another are extraordinary — the outsiders — there is a more fertile condition for a revolutionary potential to become a real, alive quality, partly because society makes it painful and difficult for them to live, and partly because they often have an inner need to think about their existence, since they don't fit into a well-known, too well-known, pattern that one learns by heart when one learns to walk. These people bear, by necessity, a longing towards something other than the existing world order, towards other laws, other habits, other imperatives. (This longing very often inverts itself quite paradoxically, into most extreme, exaggerated, 'established' ways of behaviour!)

A gay person is one kind of outsider.

Only during the last few years have gay people — as a more or less coherent group — expressed some other social ambition than being gay. This social ambition — in many cases one could even say: this desire! — brings gay people together to work for a new way of life. A life more in accordance with a wider kind of human being than the limited inhabitant of the world today; a human being who realises life not mainly as a struggle to survive but as something joyful, something magnificently rich and affluent, full of different forms and modes of manifestations.

With this ambition GLF could (will?) develop into an organic member of a whole generation's movement aiming to create a world where not only the obscure parts of the erotic map are explored and mastered, but where every unborn and unpermitted gesture will find an open room in which to perform.

...or in the World

The revolution in our heads — i.e. our changed consciousness of what we are and of our position in society — is good as far as it goes. Changed consciousness, which is partly a psychological change, *can* help gay men and women. It can make us proud to be gay instead of apologetic and ashamed: i.e. it can increase our self-respect.

But this increased self-respect will lead us to question and reject society's view of us as sick, perverse and inferior. If we say 'Gay is good', *why* does society say we are bad? There must be a reason for society to keep us down, to indoctrinate us with a belief that we are sick, and to perpetuate the myth that we are inferior, unnatural and unhappy. There must be something wrong with a society that tells lies about us.

Our new pride does *not* of itself make a revolution. On the contrary it could lead to greater oppression — and indeed this has already happened. When GLF tried to organise socials and discos in ordinary pubs in order to come out of the gay ghetto, police pressure put an end to our efforts.

Individual self-liberation may change our minds and those of a few of our friends, but it cannot change the law that oppresses our brothers. It cannot do away with oppression.

Consciousness-raising is only a first step in the real revolution. Because part of consciousness-raising involves a changed conception of the oppression and how it relates to that of other oppressed groups — ultimately how sexual oppression of all kinds relates to the economic organisation of society — this leads us *away* from the view that it's all in our heads and towards the realisation that society is unjust and that therefore we should demand and work for change. The individual cannot alone and unaided bring about social change, and therefore the next step is for us to band together, because if we unite we are strong.

To say that revolution takes place entirely inside the individual is itself a counter-revolutionary statement. It is part of the ideology of our present society that the individual is himself responsible for all that befalls him — if he gets in the shit it's his fault. We see this in the prevalent belief that a man on the dole is likely to be a scrounger — when it is far more likely that the current economic fuck-up has made it impossible for him to get work.

Participation in demonstrations whether violent or non-violent is also not an end nor a sufficient means. It *does* serve the function of bringing to the attention of society our changed consciousness and our determination that we will no longer be oppressed and put down. Violence, physical and mental, has been meted out to homosexuals for centuries, and if we were to resort to violence now it would not be without provocation.

To say that the revolution is in our heads would mean that the individual could be 'free' in prison, in the harem, in any situation of objective unfreedom. No. One might be inwardly at peace there — but to deny the outward reality of an oppressive life imposed from without is to be a quietist, a conservative and ultimately a theologian or psychoanalyst concerned only with the state of one's own spirit or psyche.

Revolution is not just about feelings. It's about power — who has power over us to direct our lives into distorted patterns and hidden paths, and how we ourselves can achieve the power to alter this.

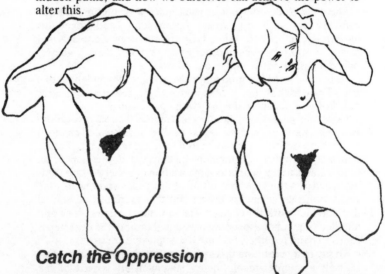

Catch the Oppression

To be a woman and to be gay seems to have gained a certain reverence nowadays, like we're really oppressed. (If you're black, third world, working-class you get extra points.)

Gay women have suddenly moved from a situation, particularly in the women's movement, where their existence was not even recognised, to one where liberal silences open up whenever a gay woman stands up to speak. Another category of oppression has been discovered, and the paternalism — or perhaps I should say maternalism — of the left stretches out to embrace us. This is not to say that there is not still considerable direct oppression of gay people on the left, but I do think that a simple 'Right on' to Gay Liberation could be very harmful to left groups and to Gay Lib itself.

It seems harmful to me because it judges revolutionary potential in terms of some criterion of oppression, and thus suggests that the way to be revolutionary is somehow or other to get yourself in one of the officially oppressed groups. The other alternative is to get yourself clubbed or imprisoned or sacked, and then to wear your wounds like revolutionary medals — your certificate of entry to the movement. This is a particularly tempting trip for lots of white male political heavies.

To Gay Lib it is harmful because on the one hand it encourages us to think simply that gay is where it's at, and on the other hand to think that we are less oppressed than other groups and so have a less vital part to play in the revolution. So either we're tempted to preach the 'gay way' — 'come and join us' — or to act as a scrambling support group, desperately tagging along with expressions of solidarity for workers, black people and so on.

A lot of these difficulties become particularly obvious in thinking out the relationship between gay women and women's liberation.

One of the great aims of women's liberation has been Sisterhood. All women are oppressed — all women must join together. Given this view, lesbianism can be seen as particularly important or attractive because it can be viewed as the epitome of sisterhood — women completely together. It is important for women to learn to love and trust each other, because like other oppressed people we have been divided against ourselves, taught to denigrate each other and so ourselves. However, sisterhood cannot be an end in itself. So more and more women come together, so there are more and more sisters — so what?

There is also the temptation for straight and for gay women to think that by being or by becoming gay they achieve a more revolutionary position. But abandoning the privileges of the oppressors, in this case the straight world (in all senses), is of itself no more revolutionary than going into holy poverty, dyeing one's skin black, or putting on a donkey jacket and spitting on the floor to kid yourself you're a worker.

One cannot 'become' gay or straight. That is to think in static ontological terms. I think one's relationships with other people, and the sexual response, must be an integral part of all other responses, must spring out of one's relationship to society. And basically the question here is whether the relationship is one of attack or passive surrender. One is not attacking the system by hopping from one oppressed category to another.

Revolutionary gay people can liberate straight relationships by ceasing to make heterosexuality the only choice. But if Gay Lib only makes gay 'respectable' then we have just created another product, expanded the market, suggested another false choice, another chain. We do not want to substitute the fetish of homosexuality for the fetish of heterosexuality.

Of course, behind these more ideological considerations there may be a more genuine dilemma for many women in the movement. For some there may be a felt choice between sex with a chauvinist male or no sex at all. However, I don't think that it's very liberating for women to turn to each other as a stop-gap alternative, a second best in the mean time. It implies that they still see men as the primary source of sexual and of emotional gratification.

What then should be the strategy for any gay movement, or any specifically lesbian movement?

I don't think that we should aim solely at bringing all lesbians together, although that is important, or that we should be trying to make all women gay, although that is tempting. We must first analyse the causes of our oppression, and if we find an explanation in terms of the capitalist structure of our society, then the only liberating course is to attack that structure. To do this, there seem to be two strategies we can adopt.

1) Challenging the dominance of the straight heterosexual roles wherever they exist, in the family, in the schools, in the streets, in the unions. Because the dominance is all-pervasive, I think that even a simple (though difficult) act like coming out is potentially revolutionary, provided it is not just a plea for acceptance, but a challenge to the oppressiveness of the hetero-sexual norm. Wearing a Gay Lib button can be like a constant one-woman/man demo.

With this goes the mounting of attacks on institutions that specifically oppress gay people. If we are serious, we should make it impossible for places like the Maudsley and the Portman clinics to exist. Never mind leafleting the so-called doctors who are making money off our backs, we should burn the places down. Never mind criticising sex education, we should go running into the schools and rip up their silly pamphlets and leaflets, and we might fire a few schools while we're at it.

2) We must attack the power structure in our society and its representation in all oppressive institutions. Fight with the blacks against the pigs, fight with the squatters against the council. One way to effect this would be for GLF groups to work in their own areas. But however it is done, it will involve us in making criticisms of other revolutionary groups. Far from deferring to other groups who might score higher on the present 'oppression ratings', we must continually raise questions about the politics of sexuality, the repression and manipulation of sexual energies in the interests of the system. We must also look for and listen to the criticisms other groups make about us. It is not a question of who is the most oppressed; the revolution can only be made total if the specificity of all oppressions is challenged and overthrown.

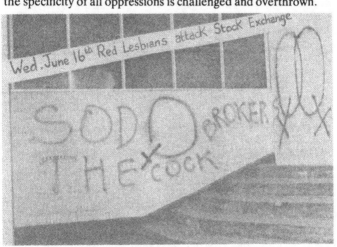

Hold Your Head up High, Love

The first major disappointment in my life took place when Greta Garbo changed into women's clothes towards the end of *Queen Christina* and took a fancy to John Gilbert. It was the first of a long line of betrayals, most of them inflicted by myself on myself in an age-long comedy of double-think which aimed to destroy the soul's integrity.

In the first act one might deny to oneself one's emotions absolutely; this is easily done in the general confusion and flux of awakening sexuality, in the unnatural setting of single-sex schools where delightful crushes flourish in hot-house claustrophobia, and in the gloom of self-awareness's dawn. That is all just the prelude, however. The action proper only begins in the second act, when the protagonist awakens, rubs her eyes, and sits up. In a delicate romantic haze she wanders alone, idealising the tender and beautiful women she sees and then recreates, and all the time remaining blind to one thing — that her emotions are good and valid, that they can be expressed in a shared, loving life. My goodness no, I have to remain blind to that because that has a label, that is called lesbianism: and who could accept for herself the image of a pathetic cold coarse unattractive creature who denies her nature and tries to be what she is not? The butch, the tweed suit and heavy shoes? The travesty of heterosexual domesticity? The situation catches me up in a vicious circle: if I had faith in my feelings I could use them as the standard by which I might measure the stereotype as the cowardly mockery that it is, and reject it; but the stereotype itself, reinforced by the conventional attitudes to sexuality which engendered it, destroys all possibility of faith. So our protagonist is unique, and cannot ever seek fulfilment for her emotions. Not recognising herself in any public image, she is thrown back into her private world. Isolation is forced upon her, and isolation she takes to herself, extols self-sufficiency as an ideal, adopts the role of a solitary. At this point the play becomes rather boring, I admit: nothing happens; nothing happens. The promising dawn gives way to overcast skies. She shivers in the cold of arid introspection and the loss of all warmth from without, trembles in the inadequacy of fantasy which seems to offer so much yet finally cheats and frustrates. So total is her self-mistrust that all achievement becomes inaccessible as inhibitions descend.

It might seem incredible that anyone could give up hope so easily, but perhaps few straight people realise that the labels they impose on us are not merely insulting, but also shattering in their effect on the way we look at ourselves. All labels are at best merely ill-fitting public clothes to our individuality, but those which carry with them a stigma can cause a barren loss of confidence if we reject them, thus depriving ourselves of an external description, or, if we accept them, an equally barren self-contempt, since in accepting the label we also inevitably accept the values assigned to it, the stigma.

Therefore, after sampling methods of escape other than solitude — hilarious forays into heterosexuality (a humiliating failure for me, painful to him) and suicide (literally painful to me and distressing to family) — the realisation and acceptance of my homosexuality, which occurs in the next act, brings little relief. I thought to dispel self-deception and find that, although some of the inner conflict and repression is resolved, concealment from others causes self-concealment, however strong the belief that one is facing up to oneself. Hence I still cannot live myself fully, and the dead weight of inhibition still flattens all creativity. Why do you conceal from others your . . . what shall we say, your propensities? Guilt. Guilt in the face of conventional values. Guilt destroys the last traces of self-respect and rampages through the unprotected soul. Guilt resigns you to unhappiness, leads you to expect nothing else as your due. Guilt puts you always in the wrong, always at a disadvantage; it draws its strength from the timidity it creates, it mocks and questions not itself . . .

(The above was, of course, written after the annihilation of these horrors. For only then, in the freedom of self-respect, could I see the pattern and unity of my past and thus recognise causes. Act four took place in the afternoon, with the sun trying hard, and sometimes succeeding, to break out and brighten Parliament Hill. Act five takes place in the clear evening, and the night.)

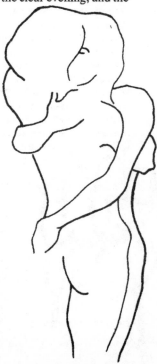

Come Together
8

[August 1971]

Youth Group Declaration of Rights

Every day it becomes clearer that the system we live in with its repression of gays, women, blacks, workers, is desperately fighting to keep itself going. This becomes more evident with trials like the *Little Red Schoolbook, OZ*, and the forthcoming frame-up of Jake Prescott and Ian Purdie on a conspiracy-to-bomb charge.

Every day it becomes more apparent that people are not going to take the shit that's coming. People are organising everywhere — the shipbuilders are running Clydeside, the people of Ireland are fighting for their self-determination, women are fighting back a male-ego-chauvinist world and our black brothers and sisters are fighting the racism of a white-dominated world.

And now, also, homosexuals are standing up and saying 'no more shit', our oppression ends here. They are standing up and demanding an end to oppression through the law, the psychiatrists — a total end to all forms of oppression that keeps us a down minority. We of the Gay Liberation Front Youth Group have listed a series of basic demands. To survive and fight our oppressors we must know very clearly what we want and what we reject. We must learn to struggle together.

1. WE WANT SEXUAL SELF-DETERMINATION
   We believe that young people must have the unhindered right to be homosexual, heterosexual or bisexual. And the complete knowledge to understand their own sexuality.

2. WE WANT AN END TO MALE CHAUVINISM AND SEXISM
   We believe that women must be free and equal. Sex-role stereotyping in

education must end. Institutional sexism in the law, work, the church and the family must be stopped. We consider women our natural allies since both homosexuals and women are systematically oppressed by male-supremacist society.

3. WE WANT POWER. WE WANT THE FREEDOM TO DETERMINE OUR OWN DESTINY
    We believe ideas should be judged on their merit and people on their kindness or wisdom. We want an end to the attitudes of the old which tell us that they know better. We want a total end to adult chauvinism.

4. WE WANT FULL CIVIL AND HUMAN RIGHTS
    We want an immediate end to the harassment of gays by the police. We demand an end to the imprisonment of gays for sexual offences. We believe that all people are created equal and are endowed with certain inalienable rights, among them life, liberty and the pursuit of happiness.

5. WE WANT THE RIGHT TO FORM OUR EDUCATION ACCORDING TO OUR NEEDS
    We believe compulsory education is a form of imprisonment, and must end immediately. Every student should have the right to equal sex education.

6. WE WANT THE FREEDOM TO FORM COMMUNAL FAMILIES
    We believe that the nuclear family is not in the best interests of gays and women. Young people are considered property, to be moulded in the image of their parents. We demand the right to live and run our lives in the manner where we can

learn the cooperation of the community
rather than the oppression of the family.

7. WE WANT THE RIGHT TO LIVE
    We believe that to survive we must have
    clean air to breathe, pure foods to eat,
    water fit to drink and products built to
    last. We demand an end to the rip-off of
    gay people in the pubs and clubs, where
    we are treated as commodities in a
    money-orientated society.

GAY POWER TO GAY PEOPLE

Tony Reynolds
(with a little help from my friends)

Age of Consent

Consent. To what, by whom, why should it be restricted? These
questions can be answered when one examines the oppressive
attitude with which the adult ruling class regards young people.

With the increase in population in the past century, young
people have formed a much greater percentage of the population.
They were at first exploited by the Victorians as a source of cheap
labour and even now young people are paid less for doing the
same work than adults.

As education improved, the knowledge gained by this large
and impressionable section of the population made them
increasingly aware of the oppression laid on them by their
parents, teachers, employers, etc., and as their influence grew
due to their numbers and intelligence, so the establishment
attempted to crush them with legislation aimed at their sexual
and legal rights — age limitations to their freedom. This is
manifested in voting age, etc. At present, the government is
planning legislation to cripple the students' union, and so
effectively control their power, just as they have done to the
TUC.

Homosexuals obviously form a smaller percentage of the
population than either young people or trade-union members,
but they are potentially more powerful because they transcend
class and age. The establishment's attitude is one of direct
oppression through police harassment, obscenity trials (weren't
OZ and *IT* found guilty by using gay ads as evidence?), denying
of legal rights and more recently in the grudging legislation

passed by a conscience-stricken Parliament through the age limits on young homosexuals. This was advocated as protection so they could decide against the perverted sexuality that the act assumes homosexuality to be — it openly condemns homosexuality through this measure as it takes on shades of the 'corruption of the morals of minors' recently aired at *OZ*. It presents us with a false freedom. It is a sly and naive, though fascist, way of continuing oppression and as such should be destroyed as soon as possible.

It violates the Children's Charter (just as the heterosexual age limit). It openly contradicts itself, for one can only be led to the conclusion that while an 18-year-old can drive a car, buy a house, vote for a government, he cannot choose who he can fuck. Obviously the government's more afraid of sexual freedom than most other sorts and thus seeks to keep it down. It is part of the campaign to deprive young people of their rights because they are afraid of their power.

This act is a denial of rights. It is a useless contradiction. It creates hostility and as such we should fight against it.

Burnley Confronted: The Struggle for Survival in the Provinces

Earlier this year, some gay people in Burnley got it together to start a gay club in the town. The idea was important for two reasons. Firstly, there is *no* place in Burnley for gay people to get together. Secondly, the club was to be run by gay people for gay people, on a non-profit-making basis.

Premises were found. The local police and all necessary authorities approved, and plans went ahead. A local Catholic priest got wind of the idea, however. He freaked and urged his congregation to fight this threat to the children of Burnley. An immediate, noisy coalition formed which included all the local reactionaries. It put pressure on councillors, and forced the owners of the premises to illegally withdraw from the contract. Their methods were two-faced. They claimed to the gay community that it was separation that they were opposing, but at the same time arranged a public campaign hinging on ancient, libellous prejudice, and blind reaction.

Manchester CHE together with NCCL arranged a meeting in Burnley central library, where all shades of opinion would be represented. It is not possible to tell to what extent Manchester

CHE thought that this might have some actual influence on changing the situation. However, London GLF felt it was vital to support a struggle for what we in London and most big cities take for granted – a meeting-place for gay people free from the immediate fear of direct physical oppression. The meeting was basically a debate between 'open-minded' liberals and out-and-out pig reactionaries. GLF had little chance to contribute and could only really give moral support by a mass, proud coming-out ceremony in the hall. The most valuable contributions were from Burnley people who attacked the hypocrisy of the pigs and declared *their* feelings of need for a proper meeting-place. The meeting was charged, not only with emotion, but with a degree of brute 19th century Bible-thumping reaction. Four liberals on the stage spoke first. Polemically and validly, they attacked the 'un-Christian, illogical and illegal' workings of the club-closing gang. After this several townsfolk talked of the 'shame' they felt that their fellows had been so unkind. Then the reactionaries got their turn. Skinheads and priests, pigs and 'parents' had united for this, and all the junk about 'misuse of sexual appetite', 'disgusting', 'perverted' was rolled off in an almost nonsensical litany. They weren't really even together enough to attack us for what we are a threat to — their whole worn-out, aggressive, restricting culture, with its quiet provincial family to protect. This emblem of respectability — the family — which must have been their pièce de resistance, was pre-empted by a woman who declared that it would be a good thing for her children to meet gay people, and if they turned out gay themselves to be able to get it together with people in a place where they could feel free and be themselves. This is the crux of the importance of the Burnley fiasco. It does not represent a struggle against the roots of sexism, but is the first stage in what for most provincial gay people is a struggle for the elementary needs for survival.

Collective Work

One of the points about the way some people work in GLF that causes most annoyance and bad feeling is individualistic style. Some brothers have been creating their own ideas without responsibilities to any group — and therefore without contact with other prominent ideas among sisters and brothers. Since we are trying to develop a more organic style of work, these people are rightly criticised. A brother (Warren) said at a meeting recently that he did not want to see two political parties develop in GLF, and that people must be receptive and learn from each other. This is true, but we feel that he didn't see that this can only be done by people with differing views working together and working out answers to problems together.

Individualism exists within the groups also. Some people do 'their own thing' or just want to exert their own ideas and trips on the groups. This oppresses the others whose enthusiasm and efforts are thwarted, but worst of all, stops the development of group consciousness. The group becomes a servant of that person or else their work has far less value — they do it on their own and others benefit less from the ideas in it. Individualism is a dying work-style left over from the male-dom competitive world where the men compete with each other for supremacy, and the one with the biggest ego/muscles wins.

Collective work is a more evolved form of work. It is based on the fusion of not only effort but ideas, and getting to the right ideas by everyone confronting problems against all their backgrounds of knowedge and as far as possible all agreeing in the end. Not because they are forced to, but because all the problems are worked through. This is not idealistic. We are held back from it only by the ego hang-ups we have from straight class society. As we break these down, collective work becomes more of a possibility. It is not necessarily so that collectives are less efficient than individuals ; this is just a myth created by a society based on competing individuals (isolated units). The recent 'office collective' argument showed perhaps that people in the office collective had seen the 'individualist' answer to the office's problem rather than solving how to work better as a collective (which maybe means getting closer).

One of the most important short-term effects of collective work is the check on ego-trippers. Ego-trippers often don't realise how harmful their overbearingness is. They're often unconscious that they are unwantingly dominating, and therefore can only be stopped by the people around them moving out of this kind of method and checking their behaviour.

If we're held back from collective work by our own hang-ups, then awareness groups are bound to be a great help. They're based on collective thinking and the strength of the group and its ideas sorting out the hang-ups of the individual. Awareness groups are a stepping-stone to collective work, and the experience of them in increasing numbers is the beginning of the end of individualism in GLF.

Sarah, Tim, Bill

Cuba and Machismo Oppression

Reprinted below are two important documents relevant to the position of gay people in Cuba. One is an excerpt from the declaration of the official 'First National Congress on Education and Culture', held in Havana in May this year, the other a letter written from a group of Cuban gays to the *Gay Flames* journal in New York.

The Cuban revolution may have changed a lot of things for the better, but it certainly has done nothing to change the particularly vicious form of sexism — *machismo* — that seems to characterise all Latin American societies. The revolution has remained completely male-dominated, and the butch image of Castro and Guevara, which is even taken as a model by so many of the straight male left in America and Britain, represents the oppression of women and gay people in a particularly vicious form. During the revolutionary struggle many women did escape from the prison of the family, and some even fought alongside men. But even here, the role women were allowed to play was

carefully circumscribed. As Che Guevara wrote in his book *Guerilla Warfare*, in the guerilla 'a woman can perform many of her habitual tasks of peacetime', i.e. cooking, nursing, sewing, etc. And when peacetime came, the revolutionary leaders made sure that women were shunted back to these 'habitual tasks'.

In 1962 Fidel Castro himself intervened in the campaign to get women back into the home, and justified himself with the ignorant and reactionary excuse that if women did not stay at home and look after the children, no one else would. It did not occur to him that it might be a good idea for men to take over this shit-work for a change, even though there is still immense male under-employment in Cuba. Indeed, this lack of enough work for everyone has been used as an excuse by the Cuban government not to make the provision of such minimal facilities as day-care centres, etc. the priority it should be.

It is not surprising that the sexist backlash against women was accompanied by overt repression against gay people. The traditional position of gay men in Cuba (unfortunately there is very little material on the position of gay women) was one of complete outcasts. As in so many countries, our brothers there were at the very bottom of society. In Cuba, as in *macho* cultures generally, the rigid role division of straight society is forced onto gays as well. A gay man — *maricon* — is one who allows himself to be fucked, and thus surrenders the privilege of the male oppressor. A straight man may fuck a *maricon* just as he would fuck a woman — without any loss of status. Perhaps even, as Genet puts it, 'a man who fucks a man is a double man'. *Machismo* made it impossible for gay men to find any niche in Cuban society proper, and so many gays were forced to lead a parasitic existence in Hanava, serving the imperialist tourists and businessmen as waiters, hairdressers, prostitutes, etc.

This of course was not the happiest position for gay people to be in during an anti-imperialist revolution. But while the straight male revolutionaries were chauvinistically sympathetic and patronising towards women who had been forced by social conditions into prostitution, gay men who had been forced into pariah roles remained the object of contempt, and were now also tarred with the brush of their association with the imperialist exploiters. In 1964 it became evident that many gay men had been arrested and sent to special punitive labour camps (UMAP — referred to in the Cuban gays' letter), and although pressure from liberal supporters of the Cuban revolution in Europe led to a let-up on such extreme forms of repression, this has nevertheless continued in more diffuse ways.

After the Gay Liberation movement began in the US, American gay people volunteered to go with the Venceremos brigade to Cuba in summer 1970. The brigade is designed as a means for revolutionaries in the US to express support for the Cuban revolution by working there for a few weeks, then touring around and getting to know various aspects of Cuban life. Although our gay sisters and brothers in America genuinely supported the Cuban revolution, they were also particularly interested in finding out for themselves the position of gay people in Cuba, and meeting Cuban gays to discuss common problems, and they saw their criticism of the sexism of Cuban society as making a positive contribution to the Cuban revolution, not a negative one.

The American gay revolutionaries were treated very badly, both by the straight males in the Venceremos brigade, and by their Cuban hosts. The brigade organisers were obviously embarrassed at sending Gay Lib representatives to Cuba, and after originally allocating Gay Lib 25 places, they arbitrarily cut this down to six. Already on the journey to Cuba, the gays were ostracised by their straight male 'comrades', and they met with the same treatment from the Cubans, although they took part in all the brigade's activities. For instance, while the Cuban men were physically affectionate in a *macho*, back-slapping way to the American straight men, they carefully avoided the least physical contact with the gay men. Interestingly enough, there were a number of Vietnamese visitors in Cuba, and in striking contrast to the Cubans, the Vietnamese men accepted the gay sisters and brothers on quite equal terms, conspicuously walking around hand in hand with the American gay brothers. Back in the US, the organisers of the Venceremos brigade connived with the Cuban authorities to drop Gay Lib and radical feminist representatives from the 1971 brigade.

The document from the Cuban 'Congress on Education and Culture', and the letter from the Cuban gays, show that the repression of gay people in Cuba takes a variety of forms. The lesson for us is clear. Although we may well suport a revolution that, like the Cuban, attacks the oppressive economic structures of capitalist society, and although we might in our own country want to join a radical movement for socialism, we can never rely on the straight male-dominated left to fight our particular battle for us — the battle against sexism. We must at all costs preserve our organisational independence, and then we can ally with other groups when our interests coincide with theirs, and break with them when we need to go further and challenge their own privileges.

What can we do to help our gay brothers and sisters in Cuba? Some people may argue that we ought to tone down our criticisms because, after all, the Cuban government is attempting to build a new society. Why should we attack Cuba, and not other countries where gay people are treated even worse, and which are fascist into the bargain (Brazil or Spain, for example). I believe it is precisely because Cuba proclaims itself a revolutionary country — 'Free Territory of Latin America' — that we should not flinch at attacking the Cuban authorities for their treatment of gay people. We cannot expect that sexism will ever disappear by decree from above, in Cuba or anywhere else. Only the struggle of women and gay people will free any society from sexism, and Cuba will only be able to progress towards a truly liberated society when women and gay people there take the leadership of the revolution into their own hands. But by voicing our anger and disgust at what is happening to gay people in Cuba, we may shame the straight male leaders of the revolution into letting up on the present blatant repression, and make it a little bit easier for our Cuban sisters and brothers to struggle, like us, for their own liberation. To the pitifully inadequate and backward sexist male left in Cuba, as in England, we say — No Liberation Without Us!

This is an excerpt from the declaration of the First National Congress on Education and Culture, published in the English edition of Granma, *the official newspaper of Cuba:*

The social-pathological character of homosexual deviations was recognised. It was resolved that all manifestations of homosexual deviations are to be firmly rejected and prevented from spreading.

It was pointed out, however, that a study, investigation and analysis of this complex problem should always determine the measures to be adopted.

It was decided that homosexuality should not be considered a central problem or a fundamental one in our society, but rather its attention and solution are necessary.

A study was made of the origin and evolution of this phenomenon, and of its present-day scope and anti-social character. An in-depth analysis was made of the preventive and educational measures that are to be put into effect against existing focuses, including the control and relocation of isolated cases, always with an educational and preventive purpose. It was agreed to differentiate between the various cases, their stages of deterioration and the necessary different approaches to the different cases and degrees of deterioration.

On the basis of these considerations, it was resolved that it would be convenient to adopt the following measures:

a) Extension of the coeducational system; recognition of its importance in the formation of children and the young.

b) Appropriate sexual education for parents, teachers and pupils. This work must not be treated as a special subject, but as one falling into the general teaching syllabus, such as biology, physiology, etc.

c) Stimulation of a proper approach to sex. A campaign of information should be put into effect among adolescents and young people, which would contribute to the acquisition of a scientific knowledge of sex and the eradication of prejudices and doubts which in some cases result in the placing of too much importance on sex.

d) Promotion of discussion among the youth in those cases where it becomes necessary to delve into the human aspect of sex relations.

It was resolved that it is not to be tolerated for notorious homosexuals to have influence in the formation of our youth on the basis of their 'artistic merits'.

Consequently, a study is called for to determine how best to tackle the problems of the presence of homosexuals in the various institutions of our cultural sector.

It was proposed that a study should be made to find a way of applying measures with a view to transferring to other organisations those who, as homosexuals, should not have any direct influence on our youth through artistic and cultural activities.

It was resolved that those whose morals do not correspond to the prestige of our Revolution should be barred from any group of performers representing our country abroad.

Finally, it was agreed that severe penalties be applied to those who corrupt the morals of minors, depraved repeat offenders and irredeemable anti-social elements.

Cultural institutions cannot serve as a platform for false intellectuals who try to make snobbery, extravagant conduct, homosexuality and other social aberrations into expressions of revolutionary spirit and art, isolated from the masses and the spirit of the Revolution.

The following is the full text of a letter from gays living in Cuba:

Sisters and Brothers,

By chance, we got a copy of your publication with the Third World Gay Revolution platform (*Gay Flames*, pamphlet 7).

We believe, as elements which are discriminated against in a country that believes itself in a revolution for the new man, against the traditional injustices that we have suffered and still suffer as a remainder of a classist society, it is our duty to inform you of our situation as homosexuals, and at the same time let you know a series of events that denies fundamentally the postulates of the social and political movement in Cuba, each time in higher crises and disagreement with what is exported as real gain.

If in a society of consumers, capitalist and oligarchical, like the one you are living in, the life of a homosexual is discriminated against and suffers limitations, in our society — entitled Marxist — it is much more so. Since its beginning, the Cuban revolutionary movement, first in a veiled way, later without scruples or justifications, has pursued homosexuals with methods that go from the common ways of physical aggression to the attempt at psychic and moral disintegration of such individuals, who to them are incompatible to the development of a society that aims toward communism, at least in theory. Here the homosexual is attacked, and this is done [by] obliging her or him in many cases to join in a series of attempts to 'conceal' what the authorities judge as an aberration or repudiable fault, attempts that go from confining them in marriages as a pretence of living a 'normal' life, to confining them in farms where they receive a brutal treatment, as happened with the concentration camps of the UMAP, which, for one who doesn't know the reality of them, were simply military units to help production, where people did agricultural labour, received instruction, and youth was oriented to the norms of military service, as might happen in any civilised country. This situation, because of the international scandal that it provoked, was eliminated as an appendix of the obligatory military service, but they have kept farms of prisoners who are exclusively homosexual.

On the street we suffer persecution, aggression and the constant abuse by authorities demanding ID cards, arresting us because of clothing, hair-styles or simply group meetings, which are rights guaranteed by the Declaration of Human Rights that, contradictorily, are more respected in societies that are called fascist than in ours, which you often see or feel as a solution to the problems of individual and collective freedom.

The methods of psychological repression, social isolation, control by districts, zones and centres of work and study, always with negative aims, are a common thing in this region.

It can be said that there are many homosexuals, intellectuals or not, that live outside of this situation. In the first place, they are very few, and if someone like this really exists, he or she knows that she or he cannot trespass the barriers that have been outlined for them, and in case of opposition there is only the risk of exile or a dictatorial system that can lead them to worse consequences.

Freedom, respect and justice for homosexuals in the whole world cannot be advocated without knowledge of the situation of thousands of individuals in our country, without protesting also the treatment that they are given, looking for an effective solution, not a theoretical one, to such problems.

We hope in future communications to give plenty of details and to clarify many situations that you do not know about in this uncertain and chaotic pseudo-socialist system.

Note: as a method of protection we have given a false return address.

About OZ. About GLF. About Freedom.

A great deal of heated discussion has taken place recently within GLF as to whether or not we should support the '*OZ* trio' in the recent prosecution. The objections (which were many and strongly held) sprang from what many of us thought was the blatant sexism in *OZ* magazine's treatment of women (and also gay people) as sex objects, subject to male superiority, inferior tools of male pleasure, objects of ridicule. Others in GLF either could not see the sexism in *OZ*, or felt that if it was sexism, it was something which GLF should deal with at a later date. GLF support for *OZ* had already been published, which rankled many sisters and brothers, who felt that such decisions should not be made without discussion. Hopefully we learn from such mistakes,

OZ carnival in Hyde Park (July 1971)

and will fully discuss all such issues and declarations before making public statements in future. At any rate, no decision (fait accompli or not) was, in fact, arrived at, though the general feeling was probably sympathetic to *OZ*. This sympathy, it must be stressed, came principally from the men in GLF, not generally from the women, who were the most critical.

Supporters of *OZ* had stressed that what was happening to *OZ* could and would happen to us. That this was a 'first freedom' which was being attacked, and that we were as much the victims as Jim, Richard and Felix. Their view was that *OZ* needed all the friends and supporters who could be mustered. In the event, the sentences were announced and the reverberations of shock hit GLF immediately. It seemed to come together in its true proportions. We did feel attacked, we did feel victimised, and our intelligence was insulted by the brutal, sadistic, bigoted and repressive sentences. We are angry.

We already find ourselves, in GLF, being censored. The workshop which produces this magazine has had to make a decision. We received an article written by a GLF member, which, for its deliberately ambiguous approach to a vital subject of interest to all gay brothers, for its high literary quality and its controversial nature, we all felt strongly should be published. But although we admired it, and wished to print it, we knew that it undoubtedly would be a provocation to the enforcers of the so-called obscenity 'laws'.*

Had we the right as a group within GLF to put at risk the whole organisation, with the expenses involved, the possible imprisonment of gay activists, and the loss of a whole edition of *Come Together*? We discussed this problem in great and sometimes agonising depth. The possibility of having it approved or no by the coordinating committee of GLF, or even a members' meeting, was considered; but for lack of time, because instant decisions would not be possible for such a piece of writing, we decided to shelve the problem.

Angrily and bitterly, we decided not to include it in this issue. We became our own censors. The *OZ* trial pigeons begin to roost. What shall we do, brothers and sisters?

What shall we *do*?

Mick

---

* The article in question was 'Shirley Temple Knows', eventually published in *Come Together* 12.

Come Together

9

[*September 1971*]

Gay Days and GLF

One Sunday afternoon, opposite the plastic consumer-crazy ready-made 'pleasure' of Battersea Funfair, Gay Liberation Front created its own fun. All it needs is a patch of grass, a sunny day and a group of people who are happy and who know they have a right to be happy.

The day before, a disc jockey on a programme I won't do the honour of naming announced the Gay Day by saying, 'Another sad Gay Day, because these people are very sad people'. If you feel put down by that description of yourself, you'll understand why we have Gay Days: they are a demonstration of exuberance and joy.

Where there is any truth in the 'sad gays' sick joke, it lies in the fact that society disapproves of homosexuality, condemns it and so creates shame and guilt in gay women and men. One of the aims of GLF is to give its members Gay Pride. The slogan is: 'Gay is Good'. The way to gain gay pride is to come out publicly, to say: 'Yes I'm gay and I'm glad I am'. The Gay Day is a gorgeous, extravagant form of this public statement.

We come together, we share out what food we have, we play games which 'adults' are supposed to have put aside with their school uniforms: Oranges and lemons, Throw the ball and kiss who catches it, piggyback rides, mazes. By these games we question ideas of adulthood, maturity, the way responsibility is supposed to be the same as seriousness, and the way spontaneous feelings are supposed to be repressed. We kiss and talk and hold hands and embrace — women with women, men with men, men with women. Thus we question the attitude which divides up sexuality into separate compartments labelled 'sex', 'love', 'fancying', 'friendship'.

Guilt and shame are the oppressors within us, but you can't overcome them on your own, in isolation. Maybe you can't even recognise them; it's very easy to put off telling friends, family and people at work, with the excuse: 'Why should I tell them about my sex life? It's not necessary.' But it is. In the face of public hostility, privacy becomes secrecy, and secrecy implies (even creates) shame. You can't get gay pride and then come out; the two happen together. And when they happen — wow, then you are happy.

Once shame is recognised and rooted out, the question arises: why was it there in the first place, who put it there? The cause lies in a society which fears you because you don't fit into its sick norms of behaviour. This begins the next stage of awareness: being gay means criticising society because it is so fucked-up and oppressive, it means being so angry that you have to smash what puts us down. It means being no longer content with the safe hidey-holes society so kindly allows us so we won't bother it (out of sight, out of mind): the pubs and clubs and cruising grounds and cottages, the closet parodies of married life, the terrifying loneliness and isolation.

To be ourselves, to express our sexuality fully, to be gay, we *must* upset the apple-cart. Gay is angry, gay is happy!
COME TOGETHER
COME OUT
LOVE YOUR SISTERS AND BROTHERS

Rupert . . . Bared

A motley collection of old suits and ties, we met under the statue of an old queen at Westminster Bridge, around six in the evening. Everyone was strangely subdued, not kissing on greeting, speaking in low voices — everyone put off by the schoolday or working clothes. The Festival was changing us into what we had come to disrupt, 'nice, normal, dull people'. A stalwart priest with a gay twinkle in his eye arrived and began to hand out funny hats and noses — Tony. Everyone wondered if there were stewards or plainclothed police watching us. Groups of us went off to Central Hall to queue to get in. (We had tickets, but had to queue among thousands to be sure of getting the sort of seats we wanted, for our different purposes, inside the hall). A party of beautiful young nuns joined the queue, and we weren't sure whether they were ours or theirs.

Inside the main hall the audience were welcomed by the strains of a choir clad in red capes singing to the appropriate backdrop of a colossal organ. The people were our own mums and dads and younger brothers and sisters, thousands of them, with flowered hats and suits, clearly all on a day's outing, the atmosphere like church-going as a child. During the singing we had different reactions. Some of us were lulled by the security and familiarity of this English scene, and others were already appalled by the paranoia they saw in it — the immense number of people, the Conservative Party Conference organisation of it all, the way the people were being talked down to and sung down to by those massed choirs and celebrities on the platform.

When the speakers started, we all quickly came together in feeling the horror of a return to the old cruelties. Things started, as far as the official ceremony goes, with compere Nigel introducing Peter Hill — the married guy in his twenties who returned recently after four years in India and was 'horrified by the moral pollution' he thinks he finds in Britain. Hill was responsible for getting the Festival of Light idea going. He'd asked God for three signs that God favoured the project, and had been chatting intimately with God as though, in the words of one of our brothers, God had been a neighbour, and they met over the backdoor fence. It was then that we noticed that some people in the audience were clapping longer and slower than anyone else, and being constantly talked to by the usher.

The counter-protest had begun, softly.

Trevor Huddleston was next, lean and hungry to look at, pathetic to hear. There were those in his audience who are screwing dividends from companies in South Africa from which Huddleston had himself been thrown out in the 1950s for his anti-racialist work. He spoke of Christ and moral beauty to an audience whose cultural conservative tradition, whether it is accurately to be called Christian or not, has fantasised for generations about women, gays, blacks, children and the poor — and put them all down cruelly in its legislation and with its institutions. Why couldn't Huddleston see this, when he'd hated the extreme form of this culture in South Africa? We did nothing to disrupt him. The handclapping only again went on longer than seemed quite polite, quite justified.

Next was Joan Carroll Gibbons, laying bare her soul: she'd had two marriages, two divorces, lived among the jetsetters and found Jesus at 51. The Youth Group took over from the handclappers — who'd been ejected with a GLF brother shouting: '*This* is prostitution!' and other home truths — and shouted down from the balcony: 'We're homosexuals! What about us?' And Joan Carroll Gibbons said back: 'It's alright boys! I was like you eleven years ago', for which she received a tremendous ovation from the audience. Then a Dane who's against pornography stood up to say that all we've heard about sex crimes not increasing in Denmark despite liberalisation of anti-pornography laws is wrong, and that something will soon be published to prove it. *Now* pandemonium broke loose . . .

Mice were released. Stink bombs were thrown. Bubbles were blown by a pretty girl in a girl-guide uniform. The Dane gave up, and for the first time the choir was wheeled in as a way of crushing protest: the red ranks rose and sang us to perdition. A banner went up proclaiming 'Cliff for Queen'. People were being hustled from the hall and the more vigorous members of the audience were attacking protestors. Our girl guide blowing bubbles was punched in the back by a lady member of the audience, so she turned and threw some of the liquid over the woman, and then leant over the balcony to tip the rest of it onto the hats below. So far as we know, that was the only 'violent' action performed by the demonstrators. There were several instances of punching in which the demonstrators were victims.

Now it was Malcolm Muggeridge, and the uproar became continuous. He loved it, skilfully using the mike to make asides to the audience about 'yahoos', although towards the end some of us thought he looked physically very tired, and he did have to change the 'reasoned discourse' of his planned speech into something much more confused.

Up at the back of the balcony, where they'd asked to be put on the excuse that one of the brothers is liable to fainting fits if he doesn't have his back to the wall, two brothers were preparing to put on a drag act. As the uproar continued below. Peter put Michael into a crochet dress, open at the front, yards of material behind, velvet hot-pants showing through, a wig and make-up. No one noticed them getting ready.

A GLF brother had been shouting about violence, and was hustled out. A cop said to him: 'I'm a Christian, but just you wait till I get you outside.' (Of such are the servants of God made.)

At about this time a phalanx of flying nuns — the same ones we weren't sure about in the queue, and who'd been warned by the organisers about disturbances and asked to pray for the people involved — charged the platform, a fantastic vision of hurtling white and blue figures. They tried to dance in the narrow space available, one of them — only one? — a man, all surprising the bouncers with their non-nun-like energy. One clear question soared across the hall to Muggeridge: 'What about homosexuals?', and Muggeridge said into the mike: 'I don't like them', clearly and precisely.

Simon stood up only a few rows from him and said: 'If that's so, then you must *really* dislike someone who's both homosexual *and* Jewish'. Another brother with a powerful voice trained in the theatre loudly complained of the atmosphere of violence, the disturbing vibrations, and how could he concentrate on God. A woman in front of him turned round and he said: 'I can see the violence in *your* eyes.' 'No, no!', she cried to the brother, 'it's the light of Jesus!'

Break for a hymn from the red choir. The brother who'd been getting into drag at the back of the balcony now prepared to come out, and as soon as the singing stopped and Muggeridge was back in full spate, he got up shrieking: 'I've been saved, hallelujah!' His voice echoed clearly all round the hall, disturbing because it seemed possible — in such an atmosphere, had someone freaked out and found God? How embarrassing in an English religious gathering. Michael screamed his praise of the Saviour, and his dresser Peter begged loudly to be told how he could be saved. Six stewards appproached from either side, and they were led away. Danish radio's girl in London, filled with contempt for her countryman on the platform, had hysterics of delight down below in the stalls.

Muggeridge was still on, after the various breaks for impromptu noise-crushing hymn-singing. Upheaval caused by ourselves must be imagined not as drowning out the speakers but as almost endlessly distracting the audience.

One leaderless GLF group in the stall decided to kiss, and someone shouted: 'There's two men kissing here!' They were given time by the organisers to finish their embrace, which was good, and some people in the audience shouted 'leave them alone'; but most of the audience were glad to see them go. Which seems odd, we think, since nearly all the men present had come along with the open intention of declaring their love for a man.

The main official event was prepared questions put by the compere to a panel of three 'celebrities': Cliff Richard, the Jesus freak, and a man introduced by the compere as a genuine East Ender — an Uncle Tom from the 'working classes' to bolster the morale of what must have been a heavily middle-class gathering.

Scene change: to the pub, one just along from the hall. Elated, high on the excitement of having braved a congregation of thousands to make a protest — it did take courage; many of us were really nervous — people exchanged experiences. Mostly about the behaviour of the stewards. We expected from the beginning to take advantage of the stewards' Christianity, and by offering non-violence, thought we'd receive none. Fuck that. One brother was told by a steward 'leering at me' that 'I could be normal if I wanted to be'. Mostly people felt that the stewards behaved well, but they had to supress evident desires to be physically violent, and some couldn't contain themselves. There was nothing worse than some punches and abusive language.

We left the pub and moved out to the front of Central Hall — all its doors closely guarded by police or stewards. As the audience left, there were those who thought we were part of the Festival, those who disliked us and said so, and those who wanted to talk. Suddenly there were cries of 'Police harassment', and sisters and brothers belted round the corner to find two people were being harassed for distributing leaflets which didn't have the printer's name on them. We started to say how Jesus loved us, and why couldn't the cop? Why was he being so *awful*? More cops arrived, two men started to kiss, which upset the cop who was trying to harass them — at which a brother kissed a policeman on the cheek. He was so surprised that he jerked backwards and his helmet fell off. They tried to take the brother, but we all asked what the charge was and said that Jesus loved us, Jesus would have kissed us, and eventually the cop admitted (between gritted teeth, says one of those near him): 'Yes, Jesus does love you', and disappeared with his comrade leaving the brother who'd kissed him all alone: deserted.

Back in front of the hall, two organisers had come out of the building and without any prompting from us invited us to send two representatives into the hall to explain our objections to the Festival. More of us insisted on coming in, and four did so. Nothing much came of it, though, because by the time we eventually made it inside, most of the celebrities had gone home.

As members of the audience came downstairs on their way out, they did something appalling in its implications. Seeing us below, with our 'long hair', our badges, our leaflets, and arms round each other, they raised their right hands, forefingers to 'heaven', and so made a medieval gesture of warding off evil. This right-arm-up, finger-pointing gesture had been seen time and again during the rally in the main hall, and only the most insensitive of people could fail to see that — together with the book-burning planned as part of the three-week Festival of Light — the technique of fascist propaganda was being foisted on ordinary people. This isn't being sentimental: ordinary people can be manipulated for evil, and that process was at work, if in a relatively subdued form, in this opening rally.

Up to 11.30, there were still people talking outside the hall. Apart from fears at the beginning, when none of us could know how things were going to turn out, it was fun. It was good to find out that individuals in that faceless mass of an audience could calm down, could be brought to talk with us, and often showed great eagerness to have words with (at last!) an open, unashamed, willing-to-talk female or male homosexual. A few individuals among the stewards or the audience were obviously longing to get at us, physically or in any other way that would blot us out of their naive picture of the world. Most, when we got to talk with them, had been let down by their organisers and spokesmen, were *better* than those that represented them. Not exhibitionists drunk on public exposure of their private minds, as Muggeridge and the compere are; not the equivalent of blacks who straighten their hair, bleach their faces and go to work in a public corporation, as Cliff Richard is; not public liars, as the Jesus freak is, making up quotations from the Bible in his closing remarks to justify his prostitution of youthful idealism to the closed-mind enterprise of Christian revivalism; not the other sort of media freak represented by Mary Whitehouse, who takes the same pleasure from exposing her person to public approval or disapproval (it doesn't matter which) as the poor genital exhibitionist on any public towpath; not that 'young man from the East End' who could bear to sit enthusiastically before so class-conscious an audience, and 'represent' the 'working classes' acceptance of the Christian message'.

To the ordinary people caught up in that dangerous gathering of the Festival of Light, kept in ignorance about homosexuality as they have been all their lives, our love. To their spokesmen and spokeswomen, our contempt for their evasions, their publicity-seeking, and their desire to manipulate the people.

Power to All Oppressed People!

Pornography and the Festival of Blinding Light

Look at a copy of *Spartacus* or *Male International* — and see stereotyped images of lifeless males with big muscles and big cock.

Pictures of the people we are all supposed to want — and want to be. And it is only because we are not like them that the pictures serve to arouse: 'This is the *real* man . . . tough, removed, unobtainable. Feel attracted by feeling inferior.'

Alternatively, pictures of young boys, smiling, innocent, youthful. In this case the picture puts *them* down. It says, in fact, that a kid's youth and innocence have to do with someone else's cock. The boy is exploited, by being made a thing of use for another gay's desire. In the same way, *Playboy* portrays women as nothing other than bundles of tits and arse for men's desires.

If the term pornography means anything at all, it means just this: *making an object of a person, yourself or another.*

It is contained not only in the sleazy little bookshops in Charing Cross Road, where it is merely at its most obvious, but in every subtle bikinied photograph in the *Daily Mirror* and the *Sunday Times*, every male and female fashion magazine. And it is contained in the underground papers where women become 'chicks' to be 'screwed'. It is in every film where the woman/man images are backed up by making those images appear sensual.

GLF recognises what pornography is. We attack it. Gay people will fight pornography because it exploits us all.

And yet we are worlds apart from those who run the Festival of Light. Pornography to them represents the idea that sex can exist outside the narrow confines of the straightjacket called marriage. And so they fear it. They are unable to distinguish between an open and liberating sexuality and the use of sexuality to exploit and oppress, since both forms threaten the very basis of their existence: the oppressive, exploitative, claustrophobic, deforming nuclear family.

And so they bleat about 'the wave of pornography', but it is the *Little Red Schoolbook*, which speaks honestly about sex and oppressive authority in general, that is prosecuted as a result of Mary Whitehouse and her campaign, and not the sordid porn books that, for example, present lesbianism as a salacious challenge to prick power.

These confused and frightened people can appeal only to superstition and prejudice, and can resort, in the end, only to the power and violence of church and state. And we present a fundamental threat to church and state because we understand that pornography and their own nasty version of sexuality have exactly the same basis.

When women and gay people have smashed the superiority of men, and when all people learn to love each other as equals, then, and only then, there will be no desire to see the sexual other as a superior, nor as an object existing solely for their pleasure. Then, and only then, pornography will not exist.

First English Gay Pride demo. Trafalgar Square (August 1971)

Why Fear?

Why is it that I, you, we . . . they fear GLF? Why do we fear or
have feared coming out of the prisons we have felt it necessary to
build for our survival and to assert, without an apology, our
integrity as gay people? Further, why do some gay people feel
that GLF is threatening an uneasy truce which they have made
with society or, rather, which society seems to have made with
them? Why do they scorn self-assertion for an apologia, radicalism
for respectability?

These and similar questions are prompted not only by the
hostility with which some gay sisters and brothers approach GLF,
but also by the misgivings they have about any movement for
sexual liberation. It is as if we have lived with the present situation
for so long that no other seems possible, or that the gay community
has suffered from so much violence and inhumanity that it finds it
difficult to summon the will to fight back. Of that community we
are all a part, and we share the fear that is endemic to it. Some
fear less than others, but it is no exaggeration to say that all of us
have feared what we think might happen if we openly declare
that we are gay and find it good. We have feared our families, we
have feared our employers and our friends. We have even feared
publicly meeting our brothers and sisters lest it be thought we are
one of them. And above all it seems that we fear being a part of
any movement which openly works to destroy myths concerning
homosexuality and to realise a state of affairs where there is no
need to fear ourselves and others as sexual beings.

Conditioned as we are to secretiveness, evasions, lies and
self-debasement — with the beliefs that we must never openly
declare ourselves or make any demands on the community as
human beings rather than as sick caricatures — the opposition we
show to GLF is not surprising, for it has unashamedly broken the
pact of secrecy to which homosexuals have been pledged. It has
asked us not to dot the i's and cross the t's, but to renounce the
truce altogether and to look at the price we pay in our present
ways of adjusting to society. The demands the community makes
on us for suppression of our sexuality have meant that many of us
have been partners in our own destruction. We have been willing
to sacrifice at least a part of our personal fulfilment and stability
to the community in order to receive such economic and social
perks as it may offer so long as we exist behind the mask. It has
often meant that we exhibit an anxiety which is not necessarily a
part of homosexuality but which is imposed on it by the terms of

our adjustment to society. We settle for what seems the safest and sanest way of surviving and even discount the possibility that there may be alternative ways of living.

It is understandable that any fundamental attempt, such as GLF is making, to break through the present fearful and destructive consensus, should meet with misgivings not only in the community at large, but also among gay people. For we are asked to forego our comparative safety and to rethink our entire approach to sexuality, towards our homosexuality, towards heterosexuality. It asks us to discard myths and face realities, to question the extent to which our social and political life makes sexual freedom possible, and to determine what alternative arrangements can be made to provide for a richer variety of human relationships, including homosexual relationships. Such an approach refuses to regard our present pattern of survival as an eternal element which at best can be patched up here and patched up there but never really changed. Rather it grasps the fact that sexual liberation is a highly significant part of any basic political and social change in our society, or, to put it differently, that much of our social and political attitudes stem from our conception of the nature of human sexuality.

In terms of this outlook we are asked to do at least two things. Firstly, to engage in a public debate about homosexuality which cannot take place without calling into question the whole social and political system in which we live. It is 'public' because the issues go far beyond the mere in-talk of the traditional gay ghetto, being a matter not exclusive to gay interests but of general human concern. Secondly, as a complement to our first task and necessarily a part of it, to question the nature of our apparently safe accomodation built to a large extent on secrecy, shame and fear. Both tasks require large-scale reappraisal by gay people *themselves*, without waiting for the liberal intermediaries who have too often spoken ambiguously about our cause. In view of the fact that we have been for so long the silent minority — the love, it is said, that dare not speak its name — fear to undertake a reappraisal of this kind is understandable.

Perhaps this fear shows itself most markedly in our approach to public debate and action, to presenting ourselves rather than furtively hiding, to coming out. The public, unashamed face of GLF gives rise to misgivings among us which themselves provide interesting clues to the conditioning of gay people in our society. To engage in public debate and action is to expose oneself, to assert a point of view, to proclaim that certain things are worth fighting for. It is, even when bitter, to make contact and relationships with our fellow men. It is above all to be a person with a sense of values, and this is precisely what we have been conditioned to think we are not. Many sisters and brothers will maintain privately that GLF is correct in its appraisal of our situation, they will sympathise with its ideas and activities, but they will finally admit that they are afraid of what might happen if it became public knowledge that they were gay; or they will maintain that they have no strength for the fight even when willing to applaud those openly engaged in the battle. I have even met brothers who have claimed that they were gripped by an inexplicable sense of terror the first time they crossed the door to enter a GLF meeting. When this happens it is time to think about who we are.

This question of our identity is not merely academic, for it is concerned with the rebuilding of a self which has been battered and eroded from the moment we realised we were gay. Without this rebuilding, fear becomes compulsive, and we have no foundation to break through the belief implanted in us that because we are homosexuals we have nothing worthwhile to do, say, or offer; one is merely, in common parlance, a 'queer', a term which, like 'nigger', at once destroys the identity of the person and imposes on him the stereotypes of the exploiter and oppressor.

The whole public aspect of our liberation movement must be concerned with destroying the idea of the queer, and establishing the integrity of gay people — perfectly natural people having access, where sex is concerned, to one type of normality. In a sense, in order to achieve a better world for all of us, the accent has to shift from homosexuality to the integrity of the person who is homosexual. Not an integrity in spite of his or her homosexuality, but integrity because being gay is one of the legitimate things that people do. The discovery or rediscovery of our identity cannot be contained within the evasions and masked balls of the traditional gay world, for it leads to demands on a hostile, destructive society for a new pattern of social life. And these demands must needs be made publicly from the standpoint from which they were formulated — that of being gay people.

It seems merely wishful thinking on our part to think of destroying sexual oppression, to think of a more honest life, or to desire a social environment which encourages meaningful relationships, while remaining under a cloud of secrecy and respectability. For this respectability is but another name for our acceptance of the norms, ideas and activities by which the heterosexual world oppresses and humiliates us. When we live up to *its* standards, then and only then it claims we are respectable. But this bogus respectability, with its personal dishonesty and evasions, will not do. For the demands we should and will make upon society presuppose that there is no need for secrecy and lies, nor for the tyranny of the heterosexual standard. We cannot demand a better society for gay people while proclaiming that there are no gay people. We cannot want to engage public attention and change society while maintaining that we are faceless and must hide the sense of integrity which gives rise to our demands.

To say, as many will say privately, 'Gay is good', and then to maintain that we or GLF should not be so public, is a contradiction in terms. For if gay is good, what is there to hide? And what is society to think about the strength of our convictions if we take up a position of furtiveness? Even if it is willing to listen, to whom should it listen if evasiveness is our watchword? Change will certainly not come if we equate respectability or discretion with merely juggling words in our sexual ghettos, without the willingness to rethink, to plan and to fight.

But some of us may well accept the need for a bold public stance, yet wonder at its implications, particularly the political ones. On my entry into GLF I wondered for a while whether the movement could not attain its ends without political involvement. I am not and have never been in my adult life apolitical, yet here I was wondering whether my sexual life could be separated from political thought and action. To some extent this was perhaps due to my own tacit acceptance of the myth that a reject, certainly a sexual reject, can have nothing to contribute to political life, but must be excluded, not only where sex is concerned, but totally. We fear making a political stand, because opposition to our views may concentrate on where it considers us vulnerable (in being 'queers') rather than on the intrinsic merits of what we have to say. We exclude ourselves. Yet this very exclusion underlines how closely sex and politics are related. 'If', runs the popular view, 'you are heterosexual, then your morality qualifies you for a voice and a determining role in public and political activities. If you are gay, you are too immoral to engage in such activities. At best you should remain obscene and not heard.'

Sex is thus a passport to politics. The heterosexual holds a political lever by which he depresses the homosexual, who apologetically slinks out of the struggle and reinforces his own oppression by maintaining that sex should be kept out of politics.

I suspect that the opposition to the political aspects of sexual liberation has nothing to do with right- or left-wing politics as such, but to the fact that we have been conditioned to be apolitical in order to survive. But sex and politics are bosom companions. In the first place, it is difficult to examine the implications of our sexual ideas while remaining unaware of the extent to which they are determined by what is considered socially and politically feasible — even such apparently simple ideas as man and woman. Secondly, sex is one of the measures we use to engage in a peculiarly political activity — the distribution of goods, services, status and economic rewards, what some theorists have called 'the authoritative allocation of values'. To the extent that what is regarded as normal is used as a standard for the distribution of justice, rights, goods and possibilities of personal fulfilment (and we should remember that gay people are still thought of as risks in certain professions), to that extent we are necessarily involved in politics. What has been the case to date is that most of us have acquiesced in the type of politics which assumes as its only acceptable basis the heterosexual way of life. This does not mean that we have opted out of politics, but in our fearful lack of protest we have become willing victims. To move from fear to wholeness, to stop being puppets and become responsible actors, necessarily calls for political involvement at both levels of actions and ideas. If it be left-wing to attack political regimes anywhere in the world which have oppressed gay people, and the ideologies that they have used, then so be it.

Of course we may not 'feel' oppressed. Some of us whose sincerity cannot be doubted say we don't. But perhaps a little examination may show that the issues raised by GLF are not phoney ones, that there are problems in the gay community and in the relationship of gay people to society at large which are not merely a matter of personal feeings, but which arise from the inhumanity of our political and social structures. Perhaps then it might seem that they, you, we know that we are all oppressed by laws, by traditional but by no means divine morality, by economic and social sanctions which reduce the quality of our lives and destroy our very existence as people. It may also become apparent that the present existence in which we are manipulated by the fear of ourselves and of our sisters and brothers can and should be changed by the public assertion of the integrity of the gay person's life.

At present what we have is a phoney freedom. It does not work. It merely makes us free to do our thing within the isolation and quarantine in which we have been placed. It requires of us that we live a lie and wade in a mire of dishonesty. The burden of fear, half-truths and evasions which it imposes is too great. It slowly kills, and leads to a bitterness which very few would choose to support for long. It can be destroyed not by building more elaborate masks, but by a willingness to confront the destructive forces of our society as *persons*, in what, it must be said, will not be the battle of a day, but of decades.

You or I may not feel oppressed, but to the extent that we think it necessary to hide or to apologise, implicitly or explicitly, for being gay, to that extent we are. And if, as I think, our apologies and secretiveness are based upon fear, the questions raised but certainly not exhausted here remain relevant. Why do you, do I, do we, fear GLF? Why do we fear to achieve our own liberation?

Ramsay

Liberal Sex Education — More Subtle Oppression

How is sex taught in schools? How *could* it be taught? Isn't there something rather odd about the whole idea?

Sexuality is a terrifically powerful force, one which needs to be controlled for 'the good of society'. The easiest way to do this is to hive it off from the rest of life and confine it in a secure little niche of its own. School sex education is an extra means of doing this: treat sexuality like other school subjects, that is, separate it from everything else, confine it in the classroom and sterilise it for academic dissection. Make sex as boring and as remote from life as mathematics or geography and maybe the kids won't have this 'unhealthy obsession' with sex we read about so much.

Quite apart from the cruel and selfish hypocrisy of teaching children about sex but coming down heavy on them if they dare put any of their knowledge into practice, this process of isolation kills off the very nature of sexuality, which is its comprehensiveness. Sexuality is like a substructure which affects everything and is affected by everything; to compartmentalise it would be to produce an obscene parody — certain physical activities with a few feelings thrown in to make it more 'human'. In this society at the moment it is such a parody that passes as the true currency. And the sex education given in schools is bound to reflect and reinforce the sexual attitudes of the society in which schools work. In other words, sex confined within marriage, sex for the purpose of creating children, and to hold that family together, gender roles which condition women and men to think, feel and behave differently so that they can perform their different social functions properly (butch male goes off to work to prove his manhood, while submissive female stays at home to look after the children and give pleasure to her husband). So there isn't much chance of our getting a fair treatment for homosexuality — which is a threat to all this — in schools. At best we can hope for a tolerance of us as a minority deviant group, if you can call that tolerance.

An alternative way of getting our ideas across to children, besides writing and distributing our own sex-education material, is to work with groups of schoolchildren who are themselves beginning to challenge the stupid reactionary ideology of the classrooom. The conference in Birmingham on sex education, to be held by the Schools Action Union on October 24th, is one very good starting-point here.

What about the existing sex-education literature? The National Secular Society pamphlet *Sex Education*, written by Maurice Hill and Michael Lloyd-Jones, hits out very hard at most of the forty-two sex-education texts that they review. They denounce the majority of these as obscurantist, anti-sex, moralistic, and vicious in their effects on children's psychological development. Their romp through the absurdities and laughable nonsense given out in the name of education is great fun too. But they write from a liberal standpoint, and what is important for gay liberation is to discover the limitations of the liberal attitude and to go beyond it. We will therefore concentrate on the only books out of the forty-two reviewed which the National Secular Society recommend (and endorsed by *The Little Red Schoolbook*), W.B. Pomeroy's *Girls and Sex* and *Boys and Sex* (both Penguin).

Gay people have been so trod on by Judeo-Christian morality for upwards of 2000 years that we tend to greet the 'enlightened' liberal attitudes expressed in books like Pomeroy's with an audible sigh of relief. Pomeroy doesn't treat homosexuality as a wicked perversion, and, unlike many of his more reactionary psychiatric colleagues, he doesn't even treat us as sick. But this apparent tolerance is no more than skin deep. Beneath it, Pomeroy's brand of liberalism is just as oppressive to gay people as the traditional bigotry he condemns. Because the psychiatrist sees *individuals* as the problem, not society. He accepts society as it is, and works to reintegrate the deviant individuals, whether he assumes that they are sick and in need of a cure, or whether he sees them simply as unhappy people who would be happier if they were like everyone else.

The underlying premise of everything Pomeroy says is that this is our society, we have to live in it, and there is nothing we can do to change it. From that starting-point, the tolerance that Pomeroy displays towards homosexuality must inevitably be subordinated to the task of propping up the family and the gender-role system which we, as homosexuals, threaten, and 'rescuing' as many girls and boys as possible for the heterosexual way of life.

In the chapter on homosexuality in *Girls and Sex*, Pomeroy is, on the surface, accepting of lesbianism. But the overall impression one comes away with is that to be a homosexual is not quite right, that we're rather sad people, deserving sympathy perhaps but certainly not to be encouraged.

The reason that Pomeroy is unable to accept homosexuality as an equal to heterosexuality is that the former is outside the framework of society (marriage and the family); it is a social maladjustment. And as we have said, Pomeroy's basic standpoint is that society is the unchangeable 'given', beyond criticism, into which the individual must be made to fit. This point comes across very clearly at the end of the chapter:

> Homosexual relationships can be as pleasurable, as deep and as worthwhile as relationships with males, but because our society is so orientated in the direction of heterosexuality and has such strong taboos against homosexuality, it seems to me that girls should think long and hard before rejecting sexual activity with boys in preference to girls.

It's alright in itself, but in this society it's not. The lesbian is 'sentencing herself to live in the shadow of society's disapproval', she is 'closing the door to marriage and children'. It would be truer to say that 'she is sentenced' and that 'the door is closed to her', but then if you take the liberal psychiatrist's viewpoint you inevitably find yourself standing everything on its head. Only that way can you be the right way up.

It's impossible to keep up the pretence that 'it's alright in itself but in society it's not', and in fact by various underhand means Pomeroy undercuts his 'tolerance' to give the impression that there is nothing good or positive in homosexuality. For example, there is the silence with which he greets the pleasures and delights of lesbian relationships, in contrast to the space he gives to explaining the so-called disadvantages. This imbalance creates a bias in the mind of the reader. Then, he heavily stresses negative reasons for becoming a lesbian:

> Perhaps, even worse, she is choosing this direction, or being forced into it, for the wrong reason, namely, because of a rejection of males rather than an acceptance of females.

There's a point in this: a negative motivation is bad, although probably only when it's strong enough to affect one's relationships with women (after all, rejection of males is quite understandable in the present gender-role system — who wants to be fucked by someone who is just using you to prove his virility? — and an initial negative motivation can grow into a positive one). But Pomeroy is really making his point by stressing this possible negative side, playing down the positive, to imply that *all* lesbians are such because they are afraid of men. He — being a 'he' — cannot appreciate the fact that women can love women, without qualification.

Or again, he advises a girl who suspects that her boyfriend is a homosexual not to reject him because of it. Rejection would only push him 'farther in the direction of homosexuality'. Why not, if there's nothing wrong with homosexuality? But of course Pomeroy isn't a 'Right On!' — he really doesn't believe there's nothing wrong, as this and the other passages make clear. Likewise, he says that the girl should try to establish a relationship with this poor kid so that 'his homosexuality will fall into proper perspective in his life.' This proper perspective is, we suppose, somewhere around vanishing-point. For Pomeroy's underlying assumption is that homosexuality is incidental and irrelevant to the individual, somehow not to be taken seriously. He takes the absurd view that sexuality doesn't exist, only sexual activities, which aren't an integral part of the personality. And so, 'lesbian' or 'homosexual' — that is, someone defined in terms of her or his sexuality — are not real beings: 'I believe people should be accepted or rejected on the basis of themselves as individuals, rather than whether they like ice cream or pie.'

Finally, his reason for writing the chapter, he says, 'is to provide more information about homosexuality so that some of the fear and ignorance leading to the rejection of other people will be diminished a little.' He is addressing himself to straight girls to help them towards greater tolerance — not to gay girls to help them to understand themselves and explain techniques to them, in the way the rest of the book operates for heterosexuality.

So straight and gay are not equal alternatives, not, as Pomeroy so crudely puts it, like having a taste for either pie or for ice cream.

In *Boys and Sex*, Pomeroy is quite prepared to accept that a great many boys have homosexual experiences, and he is far from condemning them out of hand. But then comes the crunch:

> Why then, shouldn't boys have unlimited sex play with each other, if it is all so easy and pleasurable? There are two reasons why this may not be desirable. One reason is that society disapproves of such behaviour, and a boy runs the risk of being censured or punished, perhaps severely, if he is discovered. Secondly, it may become so pleasurable that he will not give himself the opportunity to develop a heterosexual life.

This argument is so twisted that it is hardly possible to conceive that Pomeroy expects it to be taken seriously. But behind the false logic, his aim is clear. He recognises that homosexual attraction cannot be satisfactorily dealt with by brute oppression, but his aim is the same as that of his openly reactionary colleagues: as he himself states, it is 'to discover how mothers and fathers and their children can foster heterosexual development'. For him, just as for the Christian moralist or the psychiatrist who holds to the sickness theory, homosexuality is a problem, and he is merely more sophisticated in his choice of means than those who believe they can stamp out homosexuality by moral condemnation or aversion therapy backed by the police.

Pomeroy realises that:

> If a boy believes that he is homosexually inclined . . . it will do no good to 'give it all up'. This is not the way to stop being 'homosexual'. The only way to become a 'heterosexual' is to begin active relationships with girls. This means dating and physical contact, like necking and petting, and in time possibly intercourse, at the same time accepting the homosexual interest, even when it leads to actual homosexual physical contact. One doesn't learn to like ripe olives by no longer eating ice cream.

In this way, Pomeroy hopes to wean away from homosexuality those boys who can be saved for the straight game of happy families. As for those 'with extreme fear or hatred of girls'; they 'need special encouragement, urging, even prodding by their parents to be helped along the road to heterosexuality.' (In our experience it is *straight* men, rather than gay, who fear and hate women.)

What then is Pomeroy's position towards those boys who, by the time they come to read this book, definitively recognise themselves as gay, and either can't or won't be 'encouraged, urged, or even prodded' to become straight? Well, of course, Pomeroy, like the good liberal he is, hopes that

> boys that read this will . . . develop tolerance for people who may not be like themselves. A mature boy is one who can accept these differences as a fact of life and not be upset by them, who will not bully a sissy or sneer at homosexuals and try to put them down in one way or another.

He goes on in this classic liberal vein to compare gay people with 'boys who happen to have been born with green hair', and pleads for tolerance. But what is this if not a typical if subtle way of putting gay people down? Gay people, unlike boys with green hair, are not biological curios, but people who have chosen a different part of their sexual potentialities than the straight majority. How can Pomeroy on the one hand accept as unchangeable the ideal of heterosexuality propagated by the Judeo-Christian culture, which cannot but define homosexuality as a pitiful second-best, and on the other hand hope that straight people will treat gays on a par with themselves? In fact, of course, the liberal idea of tolerance does not mean acceptance on an equal basis but just a more subtle form of control of subversive groups.

Thus Pomeroy's 'tolerance' towards homosexuality should not fool anyone. Gay children who read his books will feel just as oppressed by his attitudes as by those of any ignorant reactionary. These books have no more to do with gay liberation than any other text that is at present used for 'sex education'. If we want schoolchildren to learn what homosexuality is all about, and show them the real positive aspects of being gay, we will have to write our own pamphlets and books. No one else will do it for us.

Sarah and David

When It's Mind-Fucking Time in Old Cambridge Circus

One Saturday evening a group of sisters from Gay Lib invaded a Women's Liberation social at a pub in Cambridge Circus. Our purpose was to rap with sisters from London 'Socialist Woman' group in the International Marxist Group about sexism... we had reason to believe they aren't into sexism at all, but think of women's struggle as nothing more than class struggle.

Apart from this it is quite clear that GLF and Women's Liberation have common interests. We are all fighting the same battle against sexism, we all suffer from it, we're all at the oppressed end of the system. So it's absurd that we don't get together more than we have done in the past. The LSE think-in in GLF's infancy, the Women's Lib march, the Wimpy Bar demo, the Miss World demo — these are all isolated incidents: we also need to be thinking together, formulating strategy together, using each other's strength.

Maybe this lack of coordination is coincidental, maybe it's just that we're both at an early stage of our development. But this IMG meeting — while obviously not the same as Women's Lib — suggested to us that there is something more standing in the way of unity — *pricks*.

At first we stood in a protective clump waiting for some of the women to come and talk to us, or at least to be approachable. But none of them, conditioned as they are and conditioned as we are, did or were. The whole atmosphere and arrangement of the meeting reflected and reinforced this gender role-playing. For a start, men outnumbered the women. The women allowed themselves to be surrounded — isolated and separated from each other — by men as if they were objects needing protection, not individuals able to act for themselves. The same thing happened to us: we were approached by three men and it seemed 'anti-social' not to talk. It was our first step to paradise — to what we now see as the *Mind Fuck*. They had 'advanced' from the nitty-gritty physical to the sublime plateau of the intellectual rape, and, we, being so flattered that they wanted to *talk* instead of *screw*, gracefully pulled down our mental knickers. *We were mind-fucked*.

From this point on it was submission all the way, although some of us only realised it afterwards.

Unable to see themselves as oppressors, these men believed

they could liberate women. 'How hard we find it,' they said, 'to redeem the average woman from dish-washing.' (Poor men, aren't women taking orders from you any more?) They saw the revolution basically in class terms: sexism is caused by capitalism and is just one aspect of class society. We argued back and some of us were fooled for a while into believing that because we might have got our point across we had 'won a victory' . . . as if this could make up for our failure to speak to any women.

We have known for a long time that only women can liberate themselves, but it took all the oppression of that meeting we suffered to bring out the implications of that simple premise. As long as women remain in heterosexual relationships, as long as they attempt to work with men, as long as they view the revolution primarily in male-defined terms of capitalism and class oppression, then so long are they remaining in an oppressed role, giving their consent to that role and denying themselves full awareness of their enslavement and their freedom. It is less important to work out whether capitalism causes sexism or sexism causes capitalism, than to realise that many forces go into a revolution and that it is only male-chauvinist competitiveness that tries to establish priorities among them. To allow any subordination of our interests is to allow ourselves to be pushed back into just the submissiveness and the inferior status that our fight is directed against. It is counter-revolutionary. That is why any attempt by men to 'liberate' women and any attempt to pre-empt women's liberation into any other aspect of radicalism must be resisted.

And any attempt by men to play husband must be resisted. No woman has a hope of liberation as long as she allows herself to be fucked, to live off the security of male emotional and intellectual assurance, to depend on his sense of initiative. It means she is accepting there are two spheres: the sphere of social and political functions, and the private servicing sphere given to her by age-old custom. *That is, no woman has a hope of liberation until she becomes a lesbian.* The political position of the lesbian is the most advanced in the fight against sexism. We in GLF are becoming aware of it, and it seems a primary task to make others aware of it also. It is already beginning to happen: individuals are coming into GLF, cultivating a gay consciousness, *because* they have come to a realisation of sexist oppression. For this to happen on a wider scale — such as is necessary if the movement is to work effectively — it is up to us to take the initiative.

Perhaps Valerie Solanas had the answer and was shut up because she was too close to a truth? We don't like the idea of actually cutting up men, but haven't they done the same to us? Perhaps we should find out what Valerie Solanas was really rapping about when she formed a Society For Cutting Up Men? Maybe she was cut away from us before she had a chance to give women her message.

Liz, Nancy and Sarah

Fairy Story

When I was a child, fairy stories usually ended with the hero marrying the heroine and their living happily ever after. As I grew older, I found the theme portrayed to me as reality in novels, films, plays, and various comic-strip romances. This idea is expressed throughout the society we live in, and is the major wish of most of the population, both gay and straight — to find a lover and settle down together in a blissful monogamous relationship that lasts for the rest of your lives. We're all conditioned to hope for this, and nearly all of us have sincerely wished for it at some time in our lives.

This romantic dream is so taken for granted that many of us never question its possibility, or more importantly, its desirability. But can you honestly expect to find one partner that will satisfy all your emotional and sexual needs, so that you never desire a love relationship with someone else? Even if you find one, can you really expect to find one that feels that way about you? In reality, how many people really and truly achieve this?

Looking about me, I see very, very few. I see that the monogamous dream is in reality only the monogamous myth, and the desire and search for a monogamous relationship can only cause unhappiness rather than bliss. Living devoted to one partner alone may sound very romantic — after some time the romance can often degenerate into boredom and a sense of entrapment. The motives that cause two people to stay together may have less to do with real love than with failing to overcome fears of being left alone, being unable to face up to the fact that ultimately we are all alone.

The strains of trying to keep a monogamous relationship together are often soul-destroying. So-called 'happily married' partners are often two people trying to possess each other, driven by fears of loneliness, emotionally feeding off each other rather than genuinely loving one another as individuals in their own right. Often they are taking from each other rather than giving.

Sometimes one partner is making greater emotional demands than the other can cope with, sometimes they both make too great demands on each other.

In straight, heterosexual relationships, the emotional conflict that occurs between the man and the woman is then inflicted on their children, if they have any, creating anxieties in them. At least in gay relationships there is not (usually) this problem, but this fact does not make the discord between the partners any better. Both partners have hoped for monogamy, but when they have achieved it, find that the whole thing is not as easy or as idyllic as they thought it would be. At least if they are gay they don't have the trouble of getting divorced.

It would seem to be much more realistic and therefore much easier to stop dreaming of monogamy and adjust our expectations to what we are most likely to achieve. It is very optimistic to asume we will find somebody to satisfy all our emotional and sexual needs. It is better to accept the fact that the chances of a 'Mr or Miss Right' coming along are unlikely, and instead realise that we have to make do with a Mr or Miss Half-Right, or A-Third-Right or less. So why seek out one person? Several lovers are more likely to satisfy all your wants than is one, and the stresses and strains of directing all your emotions onto one person alone won't occur.

For in the end, all we have is ourselves. We are born alone and will die alone. The society we live in is competitive, materialistic and therefore possessive! This is also too often expressed in our emotional life, so that we seek to win and then to possess our lovers, binding them to us in a way that stifles their potentialities as human beings. We are taught to look at them as part of ourselves, and often fail to see them as separate individuals with separate lives that may not always have anything to do with us. Channelling your emotional energies solely to one other person can have bad repercussions on you, as you fail to recognise there are other people in the world equally lovable, with whom you can have rewarding relationships and who can give satisfactions which one lover cannot. The notions of love that we are taught can stunt our emotional development rather than aid it. Polygamy can be a better means towards emotional happiness than can monogamy.

But of course there is still a lot of conditioning to break down in the human mind before this is possible. However open and forward-looking one tries to be, the existing expectations are difficult to alter, especially as the social structures still exist to encourage them. Therefore the attempts made at building these new polygamous lifestyles are very vulnerable, and the resulting new structures that do form are very fragile. Often they arise to serve different purposes to that which they are claimed to fulfil, and fail to answer the emotional needs of all the parties concerned.

Very frequently they are 'extra-marital' affairs, whose real function (however much the people concerned may claim and believe otherwise) is just to bolster up a previously existing monogamous relationship which is falling apart. This takes much of the strain from the original partners and can improve their relationship, but only creates new tensions for the new partner or partners, whose position is much like that of a mistress in a bourgeois marriage. Being in a position of only secondary importance to the original partnership, and realising (often too late) that your lover relates to you as 'a bit on the side' to reduce friction between her/himself and what is his/her major lover, entails a loss of self-respect and dignity, and imparts a rightful sense of 'being used', bending one's life to follow the ups and downs of your lover's major relationship rather than a separate relationship of your own.

But in genuine attempts at polygamy, for example where one lover is genuinely and equally in love with two people, the general conditioning towards monogamy and therefore towards possessiveness can all too often give rise to feelings of jealousy which can destroy the relationships. For example, the lover's partners may well be jealous of the time spent with the other partner. Doubting the sincerity of their lover's feelings, they may feel they are being used and not getting enough love in return for the love they are giving — which may be true, for polygamy does give you the opportunity of using people as means for your own enjoyment rather than as ends in themselves. But where these jealousies are not justified, the mutual lover may well be torn apart emotionally by her/his lovers fighting for her/his attentions. Often the point is reached where he/she feels the necessity of withdrawing all feelings and escaping from them both, escaping from a position which, though seeming to allow the 'best of both worlds', can often be the worst position; and the greater the number of partners, the greater the number of tensions that can exist.

To solve the problems of polygamy a greater degree of rationality is needed, so that all the emotional needs of each partner can be served. A society based on rationality and love would try to decrease the possessive element in one's feelings and increase unselfish give-and-take elements. We must learn to love our partners as individuals with separate needs of their own that often we ourselves cannot satisfy — love should consist of concern for the other's happiness rather than concern for one's own selfish interests. You cannot possess people.

Recognising this is an important step in the liberation of others and in self-liberation.

Come Together
10

[November 1971]

Rupert Bear and the Other People

1. One day Rupert Bear invited all his forest friends to do a street theatre. They were all very excited and met him at Covent Garden, dressed in their best clothes. There was Jesus with his toy cross, the Bible-reading priest, Mrs Mary Whitehouse, a choir singing 'All Things Bright and Beautiful', some jolly policemen with red noses and cans of CS gas, and six schoolgirls who had brought along the coffin of freedom in case anyone wanted to rest on the way. There was also a very pretty little fairy called the Spirit of Porn, and some schoolteachers with canes and five nuns.

2. Everybody met in Henrietta Street and there were some other jolly policemen, who didn't look quite so jolly as the ones with red noses. When they got to Trafalgar Square they stopped to rest and watch all the other forest creatures who were singing other songs. Finally they set off to join the others, when suddenly one of the other policemen came up to our jolly ones and said they were going to be arrested for looking like them. Has this been true our jolly policemen would have deserved arrest, but it wasn't true at all, my dears.

3. Our schoolteachers and Mary Whitehouse heard the commotion and asked the other policemen why we couldn't join the march. 'Because you are an Angry Brigade.' This amazed the forest creatures and did in fact make them feel quite cross. Suddenly the other policemen's big green bus arrived and the forest creatures moved away because they didn't want to ride in the bus, they wanted to join the march with the other animals. They were not allowed to move forward so they climbed up a nearby statue taking the cross and coffin with them, giving all their friends a leg up.

4. Well dear readers, can you imagine? Rupert and all his friends hanging onto the statue with the cross and coffin, when suddenly the other policemen climbed up as well to pull them down.

5. Five of the furry forest creatures tumbled down on the hard ground and were driven away in the big green bus. The other animals noticed and were shouting 'Jesus! Jesus!', which seemed very strange as the little friend Jesus had been knocked to the ground a long time ago.

6. After that, Rupert and his friends (those that were left) realised they were in a dangerous place, so they ran away to the park. The park was also full of other animals shouting and screaming things. Then a man with a microphone said, 'Cliff Richard is going to sing'. Rupert and his friends cheered, as they used to know him quite well when he also played in the forest.

7. Then more of the other policemen arrived, and hurled themselves at the forest creatures and dragged poor Mary Whitehouse, the little Spirit of Porn, and several nuns into the big green bus. The other policemen made Mary Whitehouse take off her bra in case she would hang herself, and another policeman cut his thumb on the little Porn fairy's bracelets, who was crying because she'd lost her pretty ear-rings.

8. This is the end of the sad story, except to add that the remainder of Rupert's friends were released. One thing was quite clear: though there might have been a time when they couldn't tell the wood from the trees, they all knew now where the jungle began.

A pint of Creme de Menthe, Please!

Ever since we moved into Notting Hill for our meetings, we were subjected to a creeping harassment by police and pubs in the form of overcharging, being barred and, in one case, four arrests for 'obstruction'. This exploded last month into a systematic attempt to force us back into the ghetto. We found evidence of police threats to landlords who served anyone wearing a badge; four landlords actually met and agreed that they would never serve us; and police were waiting for us when we tried. The police were telling us: *Take off your badges, get back into the ghetto.*

Our object in resisting was to expose this transparent oppression, to break it down and then to get on with other matters that we wanted to discuss and act on. Actually we attained more than this, for, through the struggle, many sisters and brothers came to understand more clearly society's oppression of us, and indeed the general nature of society.

We did expose the situation through use of the media — for a change we used it and were not used by it. This forced the police and pubs to tread very carefully: they knew they were being watched. And we had a passive demo to assert our right to be served and at normal prices. 250 of us left the general meeting and made our demand at the first pub, the Colville: it gave in immediately. But it was necessary at the second pub, the Chepstow, to occupy it, force the landlord to close, and have a thoroughly demoralised and nervous police force carry us out in a very gentle fashion. By the next day every pub in the area had backed down and we could get on with other matters. It isn't often that Notting Hill police back down to anyone; that they had to do so to us must have been quite upsetting for them.

We showed in this action that power, gay power, forced them all to back down (with no need for sexist aggression). Basically, we all were aware that our power rested in our trust and confidence in each other, our love for each other: we didn't need to rant and rave to force each other forward. Of course, during the preceding discussion and the demonstration itself, egoism, 'leadership' in the old bad sense was not completely absent, but it was less present, less dominant, less influential.

There's a postscript; we remain, five weeks later, free to drink where we please at regular prices and unhindered by the police, except at the Chepstow. There, after a short interval, evictions continued. Some sisters and brothers feel that this negates the whole victory that we gained, and that we must continue the struggle, arguing that society's oppression of us is formed from the sum of individuals' prejudices and the sum of single instances of oppression. Others think that discrimination by the Chepstow is of a very different form. We know that the brewery, the landlord and his son have tried to accommodate us, no doubt because we frighten them; but his wife has such deep-rooted prejudice that no campaign of whatever intensity or duration, no logic, no power will alter. So some sisters and brothers think that there is no principle involved here, that it is a matter for one nasty and rather pathetic person to work out in her own head and that we would be better spending our time in helping our sisters and brothers in the straight gay pubs — who certainly have more problems in this respect than us.

A further postscript: the day before this paper was produced, four brothers were arrested at the Chepstow. They had been refused service, so they put on a spontaneous demo, and were carted off. *What now?*

Want a Token Sister, Mister?

At 3 p.m. the telephone rang.

Me: Hello.

Hi, love, hey, we could use several sisters to help interview XXX. Can you help out?

Me: Yes.

Can you think of any other sisters who might go? I've been trying to get in touch with sisters all day — racked my brain — but they're either out or on holiday. You know any?

Me: What about the woman with whom I live? She's been in GLF for the past ten months too.

Oh, good idea, hadn't thought of her. Could you make it to meet the brothers by four? They really need your support.

Me: It'll be a rush but we'll try.

At 4 p.m. we met with the brother who had arranged the interview.

Me: Hi. We weren't sure we could make it on time, but we rushed. How are you?

Fine, we've got a lot of brothers now who want to do the interview.

Me: Oh, we were told that you needed sisters to help out.

We could use one, but that's all. Why don't you come?

Me: I'm not coming alone.

Well, see you later, sisters.

After ten months of men phoning up to tell me that one group of brothers or another needed support from the sisters, after ten months of being the only woman among my friends whom homosexual men seemed able to see, I was fed up. I still am. My basic response is to tell most of my gay 'brothers' to go to bloody hell. I think that I have never in my life been in such a chauvinist group of males.

Why do gay brothers always ask me to discuss with them what it's like to be a woman? Why don't they ever ask the women who have really experienced women's oppression? Those who have been forced to sit and to listen to the conversations of their betters and the knowledge that these have to impart to them? Do the brothers really think that people who are quiet have nothing to say? Do they really think that those who do the most talking are the ones with the best ideas to give to other people? Why is it always sisters like me, with middle-class backgrounds, and middle-class educations, whose opinions are taken as representative of women?

You're being naive, boys, chances are that any woman in GLF whom you know, and *whom you would feel really comfortable* asking what it's like to be a woman, isn't qualified to say shit about it — she's as middle-class, bourgeois, intellectual and capable of speaking out as I am. We are the token sisters who have learned to play the male-chauvinist political=power games that you have. What I would like to explain here is that male chauvinism is a much more subtle thing than simply

prick=power=oppressor

cunt=no power=victim.

Many of the women of GLF are just as much male chauvinists with other women as the gay men are with them. Why do working-class sisters, black sisters, drag sisters, and many others who used to come to GLF, no longer come? Off-hand I can think of fifty sisters who no longer come, thirty of them I can name — and it's not from lack of political fervour that they no longer come.

Male chauvinism is inextricably related to the values of our society. While no woman will ever be allowed in the sacred inner power circle (except perchance an occasional token sister), the ugly little inarticulate male isn't in a much better position than his ugly inarticulate sister. No one in GLF will really listen to him either. Someone will tell him rudely to shut up (last night's meeting may have been an exception — I'm not sure, I don't come too much any more), or else if he says something to a sister which implies that human beings are human beings and men can be just as oppressed by intellectualism, beauty, size chauvinism as women, then the more articulate sisters may well scream 'male-chauvinist pig' at him and silence him effectively for another three months. (I have seen this happen — if you want to know when and where, come to Media Workshop one night and ask.)

The point ultimately is that we need new values — we need a new lifestyle. We need new ideas about human worth. Not even our brothers want to be seen with ugly, little, pimply men. But a pretty young boy is another matter. Where the hell did we get our ideas of beauty and of intellectual superiority if not from oppressive fashion magazines and rigid schoolmasters? What of those inarticulate sisters and brothers with whom no one has spoken? Do you really think that they have nothing to say? Maybe they will never be academic scholars, but don't you think that their years of silence and careful watching might have led to something worthwhile — to observations about human beings and to deeper perceptions of power relationships between people than *you* (you ought to know of whom I'm speaking) and *I*, in our constant gabberings, have had?

Why not let's all of us who have dominated, manipulated, gathered the praise of leadership and authorship and authority (this article applies to me as well — I have been very oppressive to others in a number of ways) be quiet and listen. Let's stop saying things like, 'We need support from the sisters and brothers on this demo' (baby, in that sentence you just made yourself a leader). I am tired of 'leaders' who, because they think their ideas are worth more than anyone else's, think that they are leading us to a promised land. I am tired of people who consider themselves political without taking time to understand the power (political) balances and imbalances they have in their relationships with other people. And I am fed up with brothers who consider themselves less oppressive male chauvinists because they take the time to listen to token sisters while they have not bothered to liberate themselves from false standards, and listen to and learn from that ugly little inarticulate man who may never come back because he is of no interest to his brothers. Why the hell make the effort to avoid 'chicks' and say 'sisters' first if the only sisters whom you know are the ones who have learned to play the male-chauvinist word-power games?

Let's try to be a little kinder to one another, a little more patient. And let's try to listen to one another for a change — no more domination by those with the loudest voices or most imposing ideas. Liberation can only come by liberating ourselves from the values of the past. I don't want to change a white heterosexual male-chauvinist male oppressor for a black heterosexual male-chauvinist, a homosexual male-chauvinist, or a male-chauvinist lesbian oppressor. If you do, well, see you later, sisters.

Carla

Skegness Women's Liberation

During the weekend of 16-17th October, a National Women's Conference was held at Skegness. A number of sisters from GLF Women's group went along with our children and booze.

Gay Liberation, for both sexes, cannot be separated from women's liberation. This is obvious where gay women are concerned, and if you don't see how women's liberation relates to gay men, consider: every man is meant to have an oppressed woman to define his manhood; the man who doesn't have one and doesn't want one is inadequate, so . . .

Women's National Coordinating Committee

The conference was arranged by the Women's National Coordinating Committee, which was set up at the first national conference in Oxford, 1970. This created the women's liberation movement on a national scale and formulated a minimum programme (the four campaigns): equal pay and opportunities; equal education and training; 24-hour nurseries; free contraception and abortion on demand. It also coordinated the national demonstration in March 1971 around these demands.

The WNCC was supposed to be ideologically neutral and have no jurisdiction over the activities of individual groups. Within a deliberately fluid framework, hard-working, well-organised and bureaucratic groups came to assume an important role. It seemed to those of us who were in women's liberation at the time that these were groups (mainly two Maoist groups — the Union of Women's Liberation and the Women's Liberation Front) whose representation at the WNCC was disproportionate to their membership in the localities; it is possible that they saw the women already *within* the movement as prospective converts to their political tendency, and thus increasing their membership.

The meetings of the WNCC were characterised by a humourless coldness and lack of sisterhood reminiscent of the male left, which was frustrating and disillusioning. We failed to talk *with* women about the substance of our differences — we merely fought about the implementation of our ideals, not about their content. In this way many women who attended WNCC meetings were so horrified and depressed that they never returned, and some even dropped out of the movement altogether. Meanwhile, the bureaucracy consolidated and used methods, dictated by the male left, to steamroller their own proposals and sabotage others. This culminated in the organisation of the Skegness conference. Women within the movement with libertarian attitudes, who could not stomach the in-fighting, absented themselves from the planning meetings and therefore had no influence on the structure of the conference.

Nevertheless, many of us went there with the aim of changing the status quo. We were not prepared to sit passively while 'experts' about women read their papers and 500 women pretended to discuss them. Many of us were there to talk with women, to build some kind of sisterhood through constant contact for a weekend. Some of us were horrified to find that we shared all our public territory with two other conferences — International Socialists and Derbyshire miners' delegates — and our sleeping accommodation with some of the men who had come to 'support' 'their' women. The patronising, violent and interfering attitudes of these men during the conference confirmed our fears. Couldn't there be one small corner of England where women could gather together *without* men? Obviously not yet.

Platform Politics

The conference began in a rigidly structured way, with speakers delivering academic papers from the platform to a largely passive audience, as expected. This rigid structure reflected a trend to make women's liberation more centralised, more hierarchical, more like any other political movement. Most of the women there found this alienating, and some were alienated in the same way in the small discussion groups — the area officially allowed for non-hierarchical spontaneous activity — since these were dominated by e.g. academic Maoists. This made many of the women nervous of speaking, because they lacked the Maoists' fluent command of jargon and theory, and resented the crude economism put forward which totally ignored psychological conditioning and the culture of the society to concentrate solely on material conditions. Women from many groups, including GLF, felt that this should stop: the conference situation ought to be a kind that would let every woman feel free to participate and talk.

So, at the full meeting at midday, Saturday, we took things into our own hands, and before bureaucracy could assert itself once more, the humiliated frustration burst out in open protest. One of the GLF sisters (it might have been anyone: the dissatisfaction was general) managed to get to the mike, and, in a hall now filled with shouts and dissension, announced a walk-out. There was a spontaneous rising. Two-thirds of the women left the hall and began informal discussions. The atmosphere had changed at once, because although many of us were nervous and a bit frightened at what had happened, at the violence and strength of feelings, we had at last created the sort of conference where everyone could play a part, where everyone had a voice. It was not a permanent split; the conference later reunited, but by now it was clear that the women weren't going to be talked down to any more. No one was allowed to dominate the conference, and it became clear that no one group was going to be allowed to dominate the women's liberation movement as a whole.

Evening Entertainment

On Saturday evening the Derbyshire miners were to enjoy the delights of a strip show, and a group of us went along to 'trash' it. Probably most of us did this with mixed feelings, and came away with mixed feelings about the success or failure of our demo. On the other hand, we got no chance to explain our action to the miners, but managed only to cause a temporary break in the show. Some of us felt we were being manipulated by the press, who had told us about the show; there was the danger that our demo might seem to be directed against the stripper, who after all was doing a job no more degrading and prostituting than most other 'women's work'. On the other hand, the strip show put in a nutshell the position of women in our society, and to have allowed it to pass unnoticed would have been an insult to all the sisters; also, many of the men in the audience freaked at what their mates did to us in the way of pushing, punching, hair-pulling and general agro. Maybe some of them had a few thoughts about such treatment of 'the fairer/weaker sex'.

Never disheartened, however, we completed the evening by joining the ball put on by the International Socialists. This, for a change, was by invitation to all at the women's conference. IS is heavily male, and they needed some 'chicks' to dance with. We weren't really into that, and strangely turned down offers to dance. In our perversity, we wanted to dance with each other. Perversity is catching. The idea of group dancing spread like some obscene rash, and — lo and behold! — we even saw some men dancing with other men. And so to bed.

Just Private Problems

Previous to these excitements, at a rowdy 'plenary' session on Saturday evening, we from GLF tried to get the subject of lesbianism introduced on the agenda. Up till then, we had come across little or no hostility individually, but now we had to fight against every proven filibustering method in the book. Whenever any of us got to the mike to put our point, the chairwoman ignored it and passed on to something else. We were charged with being 'red herrings' and 'private problems'; a false polarisation of politics on the one hand, and sexuality on the other, was created, so that we could be dismissed as a bunch of individualists with no contribution to make to the organisation as a whole. Conversely, GLF was described as a 'subversive political organisation' which came to the conference to disrupt and destroy women's liberation. Of course all these attacks came from the controlling bureaucrats, wanting to deflect the general dissatisfaction into a blind alley. The contradictions in their arguments, however, were so blatant, and their descriptions of the facts so absurdly untrue, that they were met with a barrage of shouts, boos and jeers from all over the hall — and the subject of lesbianism was recognised as one important to women's liberation and put on the agenda of Sunday's discussion.

On Sunday, two groups were formed to discuss 'sexism and homosexuality', and these two became so large that each was divided again into two. Obviously, it was a matter which our sisters had thought about and wanted to have aired. Some were into the radical feminist view that relationships with men were impossible in the present society, and under the present gender-role conditioning. Others were aware of this view but couldn't feel that it applied to themselves — 'yes, men are oppressive, but *mine* is different, he's very understanding'. Others again did not see the issue confronting women in terms of man versus woman, and therefore did not regard lesbianism as *the* solution to women's oppression. We ourselves did not have a single agreed-upon line to put to our sisters, but rather took part on an equal basis of exchanging and developing ideas. Hopefully, it will be a start towards a full working together of gay liberation and women's liberation.

What the Conference Achieved

Clearly, the weekend was not a smooth-running affair with lots of conclusions reached on matters decided on, but certain things were achieved. There were positive discussions on the family, on industrial action, on sexuality, and on the role of women's liberation as a radical movement. At the end, it was voted to abolish the WNCC and reorganise the movement on a regional basis. It was felt that this would help prevent any one group dominating the whole, and would reflect the way women's liberation actually works better than the previous arrangement. Some of us who had taken part in the disruptions had doubts about their value, and felt that such violence was unnecessary. At the end of the conference, many women left feeling dissatisfied and disturbed by the apparent lack of unity in the women's movement. Others believed that the trauma of it all, the antagonism and intensity, had released something that is valuable, that we had broken through a sort of paralysis and in doing so had come to recognise our power, freedom and *right* to change whatever cramps and hampers. Away with fears and inhibitions — the way is forward.

(11) Lesbians Come Together

[January 1972]

Free Our Sisters, Free Ourselves

The sisters have as far as possible tried to publish in this issue all the articles that were submitted. We have not edited or censored anything. This is not simply an act of blatant Sisterhood, but a conscious attempt by us not to ape the values of heterosexual society. As a consequence many viewpoints are expressed, polarisations, conflicts and arguments appear. This is good. For too long the sisters, whilst they have rejected heterosexual men and their values, still feel it is safe to lean on the gay brothers, instead of realising that *we* have much to teach *them*. An attitude like 'Obviously what went into previous *Come Together*'s must have been ok,' is felt by many. Most sisters and brothers have great difficulty in writing anything at all, but to find once they have that it has been rejected, on whatever grounds, must be painful. 'Repetitive, poor literary content, just plain bad, not enough space', all these things have been said. Surely as a movement of radical feminists we must necessarily reject not only the standards of morality imposed on us by white male chauvinists, but also their cultural ones.

Fuck the Family

Our collective is made up of six people: Jenny, Lorna, Richard, Julia, Barbara, and myself, Carolyn. When we first moved into the house I don't think any of us imagined what would develop. We intended to live closely of course, but as we all soon realised, this was not enough. After about a week we decided to share all our clothes; these were moved into one big cupboard. We pooled our money for food, tampax, toilet rolls and cat food. Around about the same time a women's awareness group was started. It met at the house. Although the group was important itself, what was much more significant was that after each session, which usually lasted all night, women would stay for days talking and talking, in a way they had never been able to before. Soon the actual awareness group became defunct, but this didn't matter because the women had learnt to relate openly and honestly towards each other. This may sound arrogant or too easy. In fact it wasn't. Tears, traumas, temper, all became the order of the day. Long nights were spent talking, crying, confessing, barriers came down with painful crashes. Egos took an incredible battering; usually just as we thought we had reached a point where honesty reigned, someone would say something to show us how wrong we had been. Because it was not always possible for us in the collective to be in one room all the time, we decided that if two or more of us got together and talked, then anything said should be repeated to whoever was missing. This helped us to fight couples and factions.

In practical terms some beautiful things started to happen. It was fabulous to see Richard walking around in Lorna's cardigan; Jenny in Richard's underpants; and Julia in my shoes. Soon it was possible not to feel that a particular article belonged to anyone. We rearranged the rooms. We evolved a room to study in; a room to listen to sounds in; a room to talk and eat in; a room to sleep in. The next problem we had to overcome, and to a certain extent we still have to, is that of work sharing. Whilst people were still adjusting to their entirely new emotional lifestyle, work in the house had to go on. Once we evolve a smooth-running work-share system, it will be possible for all the housework to get done without anyone noticing. This may sound as though we want rotas, etc. This is not so, but we have to eat and sleep in comfort and cleanliness. It will never be possible for any collective to function efficiently if the people in it are constantly battling with a dirty, untidy home environment.

Perhaps the two most rewarding things that have happened to us are firstly, that we have virtually done away with the concept of monogamy, and secondly, we now feel that we are living our politics. Surely one of the primary aims of Gay Lib is the destruction of the nuclear family. Plenty of people in the movement nod and twitch their agreement to this, but still escape to their cosy couples, their flats, and get no closer to its destruction, but rather aid its perpetuation. We in the collective don't want to force our lifestyle on anyone, surely many different lifestyles are valid, but to live, eat, sleep collectively is hard. Seen as a microcosm it is seen in isolation; but when the day comes when it is possible for us to relate honestly, a completely fluid social structure will emerge. With a few of our friends it is already happening. They come to the house and at once feel part of us; in fact this is necessary if the collective is not to stagnate. Our attitudes towards the opposite sex have radically changed. Even Jenny, an ex-SCUMite, now enjoys cuddling Richard in bed, and loves without hang-ups many of the brothers who come to the house.

Ultimately many things could happen to us, some already have. Our collective strength enabled Jenny and I to talk with

Warren at Tottenham Tech. Lorna came out at college, Julia has reassessed her attitude towards teaching, Barbara has started planning her film; and Richard and I chaired a Wednesday meeting. An outward movement is what we are striving for. Couples in bed-sits will always be vulnerable to society's hostility in a way that a collective will not.

One of the best things we have yet got together is our completely spontaneous 'tube and cinema' street theatre. Six homosexuals kissing and groping and attacking strangers in tubes; talking loudly about lesbianism in cinema foyers may seem juvenile, but to embarrass people sexually is a good political tool.

A Woman's Place . . .

Why a gay women's centre?

There can be no women's voice in GLF so long as we are outnumbered four to one. We always seem to speak as individuals or token sisters. There is no collective response to the question: What do GLF women want? — simply because most of us don't know each other. Many women who are alienated by the current Women's Group have few other opportunities to get to know their sisters. We need to talk to each other more. If we had a place to meet — a place where we could drop in *any time* we felt like seeing some of our sisters — whether because we had a problem to discuss or some good news or new ideas to share — we would begin to come together in a more natural way. And it would be much pleasanter for new women to come along to a women's centre first, rather than plunge into the heavy atmosphere of the male-dominated general meetings — or even the women's meetings where a new member often feels out of it because she doesn't know what's going on.

Women's projects would develop organically out of a situation in which we could get to know each other and discover our common problems as women, particularly gay women: lesbians, bisexuals, transvestites and transsexuals.

Some tentative notes.

Basic idea: a central place where women could get together to rap, to organise, to have meetings, awareness groups, street-theatre rehearsals, etc.

Create: have space to use all sorts of media for both group and individual projects, all kinds of art and craft work, to print —

papers, magazines, posters, leaflets, etc., to write, make music — to express themselves freely in general.

Come for help 24 hours a day when in need of advice, emotional support, information, somewhere to crash, e.g. sisters from abroad, from prison, in domestic crises, etc.

Coordinate the GLF Women's Group — correspondence, records, engagements, notices and so on, which might sound a lot of bureaucratic shit but isn't. For example how many of us know what's in the Women's Group file at the moment, or what requests there've been for speakers, or who's written or rung for *help* . . . why the hell should we be just another file anyway?

Hold our own dances, parties, discos, poetry readings, exhibitions, anything, thus providing a continual alternative to the straight social scene.

Live: several of us could be there all the time, living communally, perhaps having some system of rotating, working at outside jobs in order to have equal free time (if we're not into the career thing).

Learn things — hold classes and workshops in anything about which they wish to learn or share their knowledge of.

Bring their children — we could have a day-care centre, which would be tremendously valuable to all involved and part of an important outgoing positive role we could play in the community at large.

Do things to raise bread.

Work more closely and develop our contacts with Women's Lib and generally

```
                    carry on the struggle
      learn      love
          live
                work things out
                       share
           talk
         dance
           laugh                  embrace
                 cry            help one another
                    and
                       grow
                       together      freely
                                     openly
                                     honestly
                                     joyously
```

Carrying out this idea doesn't necessitate splitting from GLF as a whole and there seems little point in arguing the pros and cons of doing so: it's just not the issue. Point is we're split anyway, we need better liason with the brothers, not only this but we're fragmented amongst ourselves — we could be so much more together. And if we were we could be a much stronger and more positive force in Gay Liberation and the men would benefit too.

The thing is, we'd have a place all the time to come together if we needed help, company, room to do and make things, relate to one another in a non-formal way, and generally find out what's going on; we'd have continuity rather than weekly meetings; we'd be an ongoing, creative, initiative-taking front, instead of reacting to specific situations as they arise; we could begin to live out our ideals, work out our differences, realise our potentials to really get our heads and hearts together to free ourselves: to make sisterhood more than just a word.

Love and revolution,
Frankie and Edith

Trials

In the past few weeks, our brothers arrested from the Festival of Life street theatre in Trafalgar Square (see last issue's front-page comic strip) have been tried, on the charge of 'insulting behaviour likely to cause a breach of the peace'. It is a fashionably vague charge, since the police must arrest *before* the punch-up or whatever occurs — i.e. the arrest prevents proof. It is up to the magistrate to decide that the breach *would have* occurred; since this is clearly a matter of judgement rather than fact, there is plenty of scope for pig-judge complicity.

Michael, Douglas and Michael weren't out to get off at all costs — playing it straight and acting humble and apologetic — but used their trials to make a political point. They wanted to show that the Festival of Light, pigs and magistrates are all part of an authoritarian, convention-bound, sexist system. It was street theatre brought into court. Michael Lyneham was hassled out of court after the order 'Gentlemen remove their hats' — 'I'm not a gentleman', and was whipped out of the dock with headscarf flying. He was followed by Douglas McDougall, resplendent in full skirt, dangling bracelet and platform soles.

To have played it otherwise would have been to deny our way of life. Because what do guilt and innocence mean? Only disagreement or agreement with the values of the present society. Seeing that we, GLF, reject all that, the terms are irrelevant.

The verdicts are interesting, though: Michael Redding, £10 fine, £5 costs, and bound over to keep the peace for a year. Douglas McDougall, £5 fine and one-year conditional discharge. Michael Lyneham, absolute discharge (i.e. not guilty — case dismissed). A progression of decreasing severity. As we became more experienced, as our confidence and ability to cross-question grew stronger, so the magistrate's belief in pig evidence was undermined. At first he was unable to forsake completely his golden rule, that pigs speak truth, defendants lie, but only lessened the punishment. Finally even he had to admit that the police evidence was exposed as complete fabrication.

Arresting officer: Lyneham was chanting:

　'Jesus loves us all

　Even a gay

　So fuck one today.'

Michael: Not me, dear, I'm sure I could do better than that if I put my mind to it.

Magistrate: You are not here to boost your ego. Keep to what is relevant to your case.

All defended themselves, using McKenzie lawyers (i.e. a friend to sit in the dock with them to help their defence). At first this slowed down things a bit while they discussed between themselves what questions to put, which stopped their points coming out clearly. It was also difficult to keep up an atmosphere of mockery and contempt for the whole legal process. But as the trials continued, we learnt how to deal with the problem by writing down lines of questions while the evidence was being given.

As we listened to the lies and absurdities, we became more and more angry and disgusted. So the brothers could resist the set-up of intimidation and 'expert' mystification. (Your life may be at stake but you don't have the know-how to defend it, ignorant scum!) Like Douglas telling off the magistrate for interrupting his train of thought, insisting that he can ask all the questions he wants to ask.

Our fight is not simply against police or magistrates, who are just the agents of enforcing a whole system of exploitation and oppression. They are the ones we are immediately confronted with, though, and it is worth while using those chances to point up our opposition.

On the National Think-In

Gay Liberation is coming into being and growing all over Britain, and there has been little communication between London and the provincial groups. We can only become a real influence if we have some direction, and it is important that we try to grow common ideas about gay oppression with our sisters and brothers everywhere. That is what brought about the National Think-In. However, the size and dominating power of London GLF in some ways came between us and the ability to talk these things out together. Firstly London produced the agenda by voting on a series of basically London issues. Of course our provincial sisters and brothers could not be expected just to relate to London problems in a national think-in, so there was a confusion about what was being discussed right through the think-in, even though a lot of really positive ideas and talks came out.

A few themes emerged, and they were national organisation; organisation of the London general meetings; using the media; and sexism. People went into fairly loose raps about national organisation, and it was generally felt that there should be much greater communication, but ideas which came up for doing this bureaucratically, through something like a national coordinating office, were rejected, especially from the experience of how this failed in the Women's Liberation movement. More think-ins in different places, and written communication and joint action, were decided as constructive possibilities.

In the afternoon, a group of the sisters felt very strongly that the men weren't confronting the problem of their privileges as men, and not seeing that male privilege was the problem. This came out of talking on drag and feminine behaviour. Many of the men felt that the fact that they behaved in a way not easily distinguishable from butch men was not important. A group of sisters and brothers reacted strongly, saying that butch behaviour was oppressive and puts people down who can't or don't want to keep up with it. Butch behaviour is based on aggression and the survival of the strongest ego, and it is what we should be fighting. It was said that gay men were put down because we really *are* different from straight men and we don't *have* to play their superiority games, and to play them is trying to make gay people into oppressors instead of changing the oppressor's position. The rap got very heavy and some men said that this position was female chauvinist. The sisters got very angry and it was decided to split down into small groups and rap about this problem.

Meanwhile the sisters and brothers from the provinces went into another room to prepare their ideas on communication with London.

Some of the small groups had very successful raps, where the sisters explained in detail about how they were put down by the men in GLF, and that assumptions about women's thinking and roles in the outside world were carried into GLF. Most people eventually agreed with the sisters that sexism is really about men oppressing women and that gay men hang somewhere in-between oppressor and oppressed, and that to join with the side of the oppressed against oppression they had to give up the privileges which they hold, including domination in meetings and self-importance, which in our society are the province of men. It was agreed that where men oppress women this is the men's problem, and we should struggle with each other to overcome it rather than wait for the women to tell us what we are doing.

Other small groups found their discussions on sexism were blocked by the fact that some people had completely different ideas of what gay oppression is. In one group, one person stopped the discussion by persisting that the differences between men and women are not important and that we should not talk about this. This group went on to discuss new possibilities in the running of London GLF such as social evenings on Wednesdays, where much more attention could be paid to new members, and business and 'heavy rap' sessions on Tuesdays with all functional groups present.

Another of the small groups came up with the idea that work in the community is a very important way of getting through to people and producing our gay-liberation alternative as a reality to people that they can relate to in terms of their everyday experience.

One of the main problems and a pity was that the general discussion afterwards was not nearly long enough for us to come to proper conclusions, and so the ideas that had come out were not put into action in any serious way.

Don't Call Me Mister, You Fucking Beast!

The Transvestite, Transsexual and Drag Queen group has been meeting for several weeks. So far about forty people have called or visited. Some have come regularly, some have drifted off. Almost all have been women — people born males who live as women, or more commonly, dress as women whenever they get the chance. Transvestite men — people born female who live or dress as men (if the language confuses you it confuses us too, it's not meant to include us) have so far not come forth. We're working to break down these barriers, but for now this article will be the experience of transvestite women. Not an article really, just some notes of things we've learned talking to each other.

How many of us are there? Nobody knows, or has any real statistics, but there are 60,000 people in the United Kingdom taking sex hormones. Add to this the people who want them but the doctors won't give them, the people who want them but are afraid to ask, and all the transvestites who at the moment aren't interested in hormones. The amazing thing is, most of us think we're a tiny minority. One TV thought she was the only person in the world who did this strange thing until she saw the movie *Psycho* in which the detective uses the word 'transvestite', and she thought, 'There's a word for it!'

When we're alone we tend to accept the stereotypes. By getting together we've discovered how ridiculous they really are. No one in the group has ever said, 'What horrible trick of nature has made me a woman trapped in a man's body?' We just don't think that way. The psychiatrists who electro-shock us think we're pathetic or tragic, but even those who are very much in the closet enjoy being transvestite as long as there's some outlet. We don't follow any single profession. Recently a GLF brother said he thought most transvestites were upper-class and in the art world. At one meeting we had, among others, a student, a house cleaner, an office worker, an engineer, a prostitute, a pub entertainer, and a taxi driver. Most of all, we are not heavily rouged, teased-hair parodies of anybody's traditional role. Some of us dress that way — why not? some 'regular' women dress that way — but we're just people and our taste covers the whole spectrum, from middle-aged matron to hot pants to maxi-skirt, even to butch.

The whole question of roles needs to be examined, and particularly what we as transvestites, transsexuals and drag queens can contribute to a new understanding of how they operate. Some of us are opposed to roles because they can limit self-discovery. We don't want to discard the male role just to take on the female role. Others think that transvestites can show people that roles can be fun, if you're free to take the ones you want and discard them when you don't want them any more. The important thing is, no one should tell you, as a man *or* a woman, this is the role you have to play, and you have to play it all the time. One TV, when told by a regular woman, 'You're just parodying my role', replied, 'Who said it's your role?'

There are many questions we are just beginning to examine. Why is Danny La Rue a West End institution, when we get kicked out of our flats for wearing a skirt? Apparently it's all right if you're doing it for money, but perverted if you do it for personal satisfaction.

A more central question is how to relate to other women. When we talk about our hopes and fantasies, it becomes apparent that what we want above all is to be accepted as women, primarily by other women. But will we achieve this by looking for ways in which we share experience with regular women or by developing a unique transvestite consciousness?

Sometimes the second approach seems real militant and proud, at other times it seems a cop-out, accepting the prejudiced view that we're not women, that we're some freaky third sex (or fourth or fifth?). Possibly we can find some light by considering the situation of black women and gay women, who develop black pride and gay pride, but still explore their feelings as women. Think how much more inspiring and beautiful the women's revolution will be when it joyously includes all women. Think of a Holloway demo with transvestite, transsexual and drag-queen women, gay women and heterosexual women, black, yellow, brown and white women, mothers, daughters, poor women, rich women, working women, housewives and career women. Certainly, whatever course we take as transvestites, transsexuals and drag queens, we must first destroy the trap wherein regular women set up standards by which they accept or reject us.

A similar question, perhaps even more immediate, is the question of passing. Transvestites have always sought to pass as regular women by disguising their voice, walking right, etc. Certainly it's a thrill to have a salesgirl say, 'Can I help you, madam?' But do we give up too much? How can we escape the feeling of being just an illusion, something that can't be touched or looked at too closely? And we become so paranoid when we're worried people will read us. Also, one transsexual said, you don't become the woman you are, but the woman you can pass as — which means you may feel like maxi-skirts and scarlet capes, but you wear brown midis so people notice you less. So many sex-changes live in constant fear people will discover their pasts. One sex-change said she's torn between two desires, one to disappear and be accepted as a regular woman after struggling so many years, the other to shout up and down the street how beautiful it is to be transsexual. If you're young and haven't suffered as much, you're quick to say be militant, don't hide. Those who came out long ago are often the proudest because they've been themselves the longest. But they also know that if you pass you're treated as a human being, if you don't you're treated as a pervert or a roadshow.

Yet there are also thrills to not passing, or more precisely, not caring if you pass. You dress, comb your hair, use make-up to suit yourself, not to go unnoticed. And you discover yourself developing street instincts: how to handle crowds, how to judge people approaching you, what to do about police. One sister always carries an Italian women's magazine on the tube so if someone speaks to her she can wave the magazine and pretend she doesn't speak English. You learn to laugh at people before they laugh at you. You become your own street theatre. Two transvestites can conquer a whole department store of uptight straight people.

Certainly one thing becomes more and more clear as we come together; pass or not pass, we can't let anybody tell us what we are. One sister said that after six months of psychiatric treatment she discovered that no one knew her like herself. We can't let anybody tell us we're men, when we know we're women. As Holly Woodlawn once said in New York, 'Don't call me mister, you fucking beast!'

Some people whose ideas or experience are reflected in this article are: Roz, Paula, Rachel, Della, Edith, Susan, Perry, Patty, Christine.

On Going Out Alone in Drag for the First Time

Let us suppose you have been 'dragging' privately for some time, and that you have been to a few public events — say fancy-dress dances — dressed as a woman, arriving by private car, or taxi, and leaving the same way. This means that you have not yet taken the risk of walking down a street, getting on a bus or train, or being seen by the ordinary public in female dress.

From this one can infer that you are used to the application and wearing of make-up and are sufficiently confident in your dress sense to make your first solo attempt to run the 'sex barrier'. You have probably spent some dreadful moments contemplating this outing, and trying to summon up enough nerve to see it through.

However, each time you reflect upon the 'expedition', the madder it seems, yet you're determined to try it just the same.

Now each case is different, but for the majority of TVs, the first encounter with the general public is bound to be a spine-chilling affair, especially in the vicinity of a shopping centre, a bus queue, on the underground, or in any well-lit spot. So although I cannot think of any means of sparing you icicles down your spine, I can, as one who has learnt the hard way, give one or two hints that might prevent you 'coming a cropper'.

It is very easy for those who have never been out in female dress alone to say, 'Behave naturally', 'Walk without mincing or wiggling, etc.', but even if one has a natural female-type walk, there are a heap of mistakes one can make in public. One of the easiest traps to fall into is likely to occur in a bus queue. Most men have been brought up to always allow a woman passenger to precede them on mounting a vehicle. So it is quite easy to forget that you are supposed to be a female, and let some woman who has planted herself alongside of you in the queue jump onto the bus first. This is of course quite correct behaviour if you are dressed as a man, but when in drag it will more likely earn you a searching look from the conductor or conductress, and an even worse one when your fare is taken — it might even get you called 'sir', instead of 'dear'.

Another thing to bear in mind in dealing with public servants or conveyances, and otherwise, is to use short sentences and keep your voice down. In this way, some of its male overtones will be drowned by the sound of the street or that of the vehicle. A good trick for the first trip on the underground is to purchase your ticket earlier in the day (whilst wearing male clothes) and use it later, when in drag, in the evening. Here, however, a note of warning must be uttered. Never, on any account, attempt to use your everyday season ticket when in drag — there are certain private ciphers on these tickets which indicate the sex of the holder. This might seem obvious to some, but it very nearly exposed me to ridicule.

Another thing that might seem obvious to some is that it is very important to time your journey. In fact, unless your destination is that of a friend's house or flat, where of course a 'neutral' toilet is available, it is safest to limit your first solo excursion to about half an hour or so, unless you are prepared to endure acute physical discomfort all the way home. Always make sure that your friends are at home by phoning first if possible; and if by sheer bad luck they don't answer the bell when you arrive, then immediately make for the nearest bus stop or railway station, even if it means calling a taxi to get there quickly. There are of course many brave TVs who venture down women's toilets in full drag, but it would be disastrous for a first-time-outer to attempt this, unless he wants to be involved in a criminal prosecution.

Another risk that one in drag is likely to face is losing one's way. So first make sure you are au fait with the streets near your destination by studying a map of the district beforehand, or, better still, slip an *A-Z* into your handbag. This will spare you the embarrassment of approaching complete strangers for directions; these people might quite possibly see through your disguise, and bring you down with an over-emphasised 'sir'. On the subject of strangers, there is of course the risk of an attempted pick-up, especially where drunks are concerned. I have found that one ruse is successful in dealing with these people, or in fact in any case where one wishes to avoid conversation, and that is to take a foreign periodical with you and pretend to read it. Then, if an obviously unpleasant person tries to start a conversation, just say 'noa unnerstan', in the most broken English imaginable.

These are of course only a few of the pitfalls that face one on a solo journey on public transport in drag, but they are certainly the most likely to occur. Of course, confidence is everything, as with most things, and this only comes with practice. Most other problems come under the headings of dress, style, deportment, make-up, etc., which of course one should attempt to master before venturing out alone.

It would fill a book to cover all these in detail, and fortunately this has been done already by a talented woman sex-change Ph.D., living in the USA. Entitled *How To Be a Woman Although Male*, it can be obtained from several publisher's agents, notably from the proprietors of the Continental Shoe Shop, Westbourne Grove, London.

In this very brief article I have tried to cover some of the difficulties facing those planning their first solo venture. But should any reader require further advice or information, I will do my level best to help. One should write to me, care of the editors of this periodical, enclosing a stamped addressed envelope.

Meanwhile, let me wish you the best of luck on your first trip alone.

Paula

Come Together

12

[*March 1972*]

The Twilight World of the Heterosexual

In this enlightened frank age we must all face the fact that, like it or not, heterosexuals make up a sizeable portion of the population. Since by their very nature heterosexuals are furtive and deceptive, no one can say for sure exactly how many there are, but psychiatric estimates run from 5 to 20 per cent in England and America and slightly higher in Europe. We have no figures at all for the Orient, since inscrutability added to furtiveness makes it impossible to judge.

Outwardly Normal

While many people naïvely think that heterosexuals are easily recognised, the reverse is often the case, for in reality very few are the close-cropped snarling man or the simpering passive woman we see in the movies. Many lead outwardly normal lives, and the gentle boy next door and the tough competent girl down the street may have more than a passing interest in each other.

What then is heterosexuality? Simply put, it is the inability to love your own sex and the subsequent turning for sexual release to the opposite sex. Many hardened heterosexuals will attempt to turn it round and insist that heterosexuality is the ability to love the *opposite* sex. But if this were true, it would have to be an ability that grew out of a complete homosexual fulfilment — for it stands to reason that you can't love something different to yourself unless you can first love people the same as you. And most heterosexuals are incapable of a true homosexual relationship.

Strange Rituals

The claim that heterosexuality involves *love* falls apart when we examine the nature of heterosexual activities. There are two forms of heterosexual union, the 'affair' and the 'marriage'. In both, the sexual activities themselves are mechanical, non-feeling, unrelated to the individual couple, and prescribed in advance according to the strange rituals of the heterosexual twilight world. The man has certain things he is supposed to do in a certain order, and the woman likewise. It is difficult for the healthy homosexual to grasp how alienating heterosexual 'love' really is, but perhaps we can glimpse it when we examine that curious artefact, the sex manual. These are books, and the heterosexual world abounds with literally hundreds of them, that actually describe, step by step, the actions that heterosexuals are supposed to perform when they 'make love'.

It is hard to say whether the 'affair' or the 'marriage' is more artificial and restrictive. In the first, the man and woman will meet, perhaps in the notorious 'cocktail bars' with their cold hushed atmosphere, so different from the lively gay bars most of us know. Then they will 'chat', a process which consists of talking inanely about any subject so long as they do not reveal any part of their personalities. In fact, the entire 'affair' consists of projecting a false image, obtaining the prescribed release, and then breaking off relations.

Special Hotels

When the proper time has elapsed the man and woman will go off to a special hotel maintained especially for heterosexual liaisons. There they will each do what their manual tells them and then say goodbye, priding themselves that they have never betrayed any real emotion. Perhaps they will meet again and repeat the process, perhaps not.

The 'marriage' is a much more bizarre form of practice and one which is far too complicated to describe here. Briefly considered, it is an agreement between two heterosexuals to live together for the rest of their lives and never relate sexually to anyone but each other. Though we might think such a stange arrangement might at least produce some degree of honesty, the opposite is often the case, as the heterosexual compulsion to project totally false images becomes more and more obsessive over the years.

Hormonal Imbalance

What causes a woman or a man to stray so far from normal development? To date, medical authorities have not developed any comprehensive theory. While some doctors claim a hormonal imbalance, many psychiatrists consider it an over-identification with the mother or father or both. One interesting theory claims that insecurity makes the woman want her vagina engorged or the man want his penis sheathed. Perhaps some engaged in their first heterosexual acts as a form of rebellion and then, guilt-ridden, felt they were trapped in the heterosexual world for ever.

One thing is certain. The problem will not go away by our pretending it does not exist. Nor will making heterosexuality a crime deter those men and women from seeking each other out and arranging their secret liaisons. We who are more fortunate must learn compassion for those who cannot help themselves, who do not choose to be this way (though many will exhibit a reverse stubborn pride). If we do not close our eyes, if in fact we can devote more extensive research into the whole range of human sexuality, then perhaps we can eventually release the diverse sexual elements in all of us and restore these unfortunate people to society.

Rachel Pollack

Shirley Temple Knows

Kneel on a cool stone floor covered with the sperm of innumerable, beautiful men, and hold an eight-inch prick while your brother holds yours. Watch two men fucking and smell the shit smeared over the walls, or be watched while some mighty stud fucks you. Sex without the embarrassments of individuality, the oppressions of class, the codes of clothing and fetish, pure anarchic, ecstatic sex. Have just a head appear under a partition and chew your balls, or four middle-aged men grope and lick while you wank, or a schoolboy's prick in your mouth, or an old man's tongue up your bum. Time was when I could not have endured the office on an afternoon so grey, so muggy, so rain-slanty as this. The history of human relationships is lived through and replaced in the cubicles. The pretensions of long-term meaningful relationships are swamped by passionate immediate sex.

This area of experience is the most exciting battleground of the sexual revolution. My mind would have reached out for the sweeter and more tranquil places... for azure skies and coral beaches... In an ordinary relationship, homosexuals and the rest indulge themselves in all the small pains and pleasures of interdependence and emotional blackmail, call it love, and look for sex without complications elsewhere. I walk in the door knowing that I am expected, that ears are listening and cocks waiting in the cubicles that face me. I glance lovingly in the mirror, whatever I look like doesn't matter now where everyone is equal, and only lust, daring and cunning count. I remembered the uplift of my heart at the sight of him, so tall, so fresh, an air of youth mingled with maturity suggested by the greying hair at his temples. Take away the complications and you take away the love relationship. The cubicles are all full, so I wait and watch the wankers and the straights dribble their piss into porcelain lips, with a sneer of certain victory on my face — this is my jungle. I loved him for his thoughtful frowning after the exact phrase, and for the way he rocked in his swivel chair with careless grace . . . Break out of the prison called 'love', with its inevitable misunderstanding of each other's experience.

I bang loudly on all the doors, causing a small flurry of toilet paper, and bare knees to rise from the floor. He looked at me kindly and continued, 'How do you like being in the typing pool?' When you love, sex becomes distorted to carry messages about ego situations, and not about itself. When the straights leave, I look through the small holes in the door, and can see their beautiful cocks, proudly displayed, large white bums pointing to heaven, and sometimes gobs of cum flying through the air, laden with the incense smell of disinfectant. 'I like it', I began slowly, 'because I see lots of people and get a wide view of the firm's activities, but I'd rather be one man's secretary' — I had paused and smiled — 'if he was nice'.

Our lust is dispersed in attempts to lay defensive fantasies on each other. Finally a nervous queen has an orgasm, wipes his thighs and comes out, he ignores me and goes to wash his hands, satiated and wise. I pull the paper from the holes, bolt the door and drop my trousers, no knickers — we begin.

I went to glossy magazines for advice, and followed it. Ten minute stretches in the morning. A new hair-do to compliment my oval face. Crisp, fresh blouses, skirts that a nightly iron made wrinkle-free. Instinct urged me not only to please my boss but to satisfy him too. On my left is a young boy about 20, with blue eyes, brown hair long and curly, tanned face, a muscular body and a cock that is large, stiff and ready for action. Get out of so-called 'love relationships' and into sex, fuck in toilets, have endless one-night stands, make yourself an unmistakeable and invincible sex object. The boy uses another guy's cum for lubrication, and it works beautifully . . . his eyebrows shot aloft in the way I loved . . . he watches as I rub my erect prick slowly, and so does the man on the other side. I handled my thoughts with care. There would be time enough for those pictures at the back of my mind to come true. He is about 45, stripped of his tweed coat, sports shirt and tie, and is wearing flesh-coloured tights, black panties and a black bra, which allows his tits to fall through, mock dugs, he's on hormones. Only desire to act and experience, don't desire another's experience. Afterwards there came smiles. There were little jokes. The younger guy puts his hand under, I kneel down and we grope each other's cocks, his feels enormous. 'It's no use; I can't go on like this. Until you came I was lonely — feeling nothing, wishing nothing.' The other guy reaches under and strokes my arse. I am so excited it's all I can do not to come immmediately. You've breathed life into me . . . you've breathed love. I can see the whole scene reflected perfectly on the shiny black walls. Time doesn't deepen a relationship; it allows you to record its slow death, and accept habit instead of love. You're better off to wank, with a bottle up your arse. And there was another picture I loved. Of driving through the rain in his shiny black car. Of nestling against him. Of guiding him in a soft, excited voice, 'It's the next turning on the left, darling'. Suddenly the young boy shoots, and he places my hand so it catches the warm cream from his cock. I wrap the white juice around my prick and squeeze his hand onto it. He holds me as I lead him into the lounge, and Dad rises slowly from the leather chair by the fire, Mother looks sweet and sage as I call, 'I've brought him in to say hello'. The other guy slips his finger up my bum. Later, when the sound of the car had gone, Dad looks round from his evening paper, and murmurs over his shoulder, 'You're a lucky boy, my darling, darling, darling . . . will you marry me?' And in that instant, in that dizzy, whirling, heart-pounding instant . . . Joy. I can feel two pairs of hands caressing my body as it dissolves into orgasm, and my cum sprays over my reflection on the wall. My day in the cottage has begun. Under the noses of the straights, in the middle of their palace, we make love.

The Harrow Witch-Hunt: Just Like the Bad Old Days

Every day of the week, Saturdays and Sundays included, gay people are unjustly arrested for soliciting, loitering, importuning and indecency. Very rarely do the charges get defended in the courts, let alone challenged; most victims cannot afford the money, the time, or the publicity. The magistrates will always accept the stories cooked up by the police, in the face of the most blatant lying on their part, because they believe that there's 'no smoke without fire' — such are the 'legal brains' who rule the Bench.

Yet most cases involve policemen acting as either 'agents provocateurs' deliberately trying to lead gay people on by posing as gays, or as spies, in closets on railway stations, in the doorways of public lavatories or behind bushes in public parks. Always they tell the courts of complaints from members of the public — never do they produce them as witnesses. Not only do the police enjoy, in their perverted fashion, this kind of work; they positively thrive on it by boosting their record of arrests, and frequently by lining their pockets.

Three brothers in GLF in the past year have been forced by pairs of 'plainclothed' card-carrying cops to part with all their money, after being grabbed while leaving loos and threatened with charges. Harrow police boast of 108 gay arrests last year from the same two cottages. A gay brother reports seeing three cops, dressed in what they apparently imagined to be a gay fashion, around one of these loos; one enticed him inside, then all three arrested him. These random cases from the local papers tell of the misery and persecution wrought by those pigs out of their sick, twisted minds.

The hypocrisy of a so-called liberal society which claims to allow men to be homosexual, but determinedly prevents them from contacting each other by any means, whilst allowing heterosexuals to go to extremes of so-called permissiveness, could not be more glaringly demonstrated than it has been in Harrow in the past couple of years.

Since the 1967 Sexual Offences Act (the so-called 'queers' charter' as it was described by its more fanatic opponents), arrests have increased to ludicrous proportions. So much for the supposed freedom gay men were led to expect. So much for paper laws!

Every gay person must decide that his freedom has to be fought for and defended. First he must free himself from guilt and learn to feel Gay Pride. The ways in which we make love are not dirty, or sinful, though fascist moralists may call us criminals.

If you are arrested — *say nothing!*

Do not plead guilty; defend yourself.

Do not be sweet-talked by police or solicitors into admitting offences. If found guilty, appeal.

Do not pay the fines imposed — fight back.

If you feel alone, call us, we will advise and help you. Not to pay your fines, but to help you fight back, and regain your gay pride.

Mick

The Myth of Sexual Attraction

If people are going to clear all the sexist shit out of their heads once and for all, they have to go to the root of the problem and destroy the idea of sexual attraction, since it is this idea that underpins the whole sexist structure. It causes people to classify others as pretty or ugly (a revolting kind of elitism), decide they want them sexually, go cruising, go cottaging, seek casual sex, place sex-centred small ads, and uphold romantic love (which is based on the notion that each partner is the most sexually attractive person the other has met).

Few people seem to realise that sexual attraction is a hallucination, a type of hero/heroine worship that doesn't see people as real people, with all their faults and rough edges, but projects an ideal image onto them that imagines they are in some way perfect, unique or extraordinary. People believe that certain faces, cocks, breasts, body shapes etc. really are perfect, and somehow fail to notice all the warts, moles, bumps, lumps and eczema that are there as well. People declare that certain movements and gestures are unsurpassable, and completely overlook the moments of clumsiness and hesitation. It is a kind of fetishism whereby people cannot love others simply for what they are, and relate to them sexually as part of that love, but have to be artificially stimulated into relating to them on the basis of a superimposed fantasy. Like other types of fetishism, it is preoccupied with sex rather than love.

As a result of long conditioning, the process of slotting these ideal images onto people who very vaguely approximate to them has become so automatic that people no longer realise they are doing it, and they now confuse the illusion with reality. Once this illusion of sexual attraction is nailed, people can stop saying that they 'fancy' X, that he/she is 'rather pretty', that they 'wouldn't kick him/her out of bed', that he/she 'turns them on', and so forth, and they can start summing people up in mental and emotional terms rather than physical terms — X is interesting, or intelligent, or gentle, or sympathetic, or whatever.

This straight away undermines any obsession with sex for sex's sake, and collapses the secondary sexist structures of cruising, cottaging etc. Because it brings the realisation that no person is more 'sexually attractive' than another, and that all people have an equally valid identity, the perverted desire for romantic love, for a permanent fixation on one particular person, is seen as ridiculous. Equally, the desire for casual sex, which involves the exactly opposite perversion of wanting no permanent fixations whatever and treating people simply as a throwaway sexual commodity, disappears since no one is seen as sexually attractive and there is no interest in simply going to bed wth them. With these two perversions out of the way, the road is clear for a progression to non-sexist communal love, where people can freely show mental, emotional and physical love to everyone without thinking in terms either of endless fixations or no fixations, but simply in terms of giving love whenever it's needed to whoever needs it.

Nick

Come Together (Camden) 13

[*April 1972*]

About Us

Camden is a very large North London borough, with nearly a quarter of a million people of varying social class, race, and ethnic group. As in all central London boroughs, there is a large floating population of young single people, many of them gay. Camden GLF started in Camden simply because people who felt strongly about local groups lived there.

It isn't exactly a gay ghetto like Earl's Court, but it does include well-known gay haunts and a few gay pubs — no doubt you have all heard of Hampstead Heath. Most gay people who live in Camden have to go elsewhere for their social life — there are no clubs for gay people, and the pubs are very straight.

Our group was meant to be a response to this local area; the majority of our aims and actions are orientated towards providing an alternative for gay people in the area. This is not just on a social level, which we recognise as being of prime importance, but on a level which creates gay consciousness and pride, so leading, we hope, to a new gay lifestyle and sense of community.

This issue, as it is produced in Camden, is mainly about Camden, both inside our group and outside. In this article we're just talking about the social scene and what we are trying to do to improve it.

We have two quite well-known gay pubs — the Black Cap in Camden High St. and the William IV in Hampstead High St. The Black Cap specialises in drag, and the people who go there tend to be more working-class, as Camden Town is a working-class area. The William IV is just the opposite. No drag, very respectable, polite conversation, lots of middle-class gays and a heavy atmosphere to those of us who have experienced greater freedom. Both these pubs, despite their class differences, are highly exploitative of gay people. GLF has been thrown out of both for leafleting and selling *Come Together*. Because gay people have hardly anywhere else to go to, the landlords charge higher prices than usual for drinks — the same old story.

Trying to present an alternative to this scene has many problems. For a start we would like to put on regular dances as West London group is doing, also weekly discos, but Camden council blacklisted GLF because of an incident at an earlier GLF dance. And we haven't yet managed to find a pub or hall that would let us hold a disco. In a way this has given us time for thought about the nature of the dances and discos put on before by GLF. We still use straight music and dance styles, but we hope to learn from past mistakes. When we do get our dances together we'll be using lots of theatre and gay dance styles — it won't be a straight event.

Because we could not put on a disco of our own, we started going to a straight disco next door to the hall where we meet in Kentish Town, after the Thursday meetings. It was frequented by black and white working-class young people. Immediately, GLF's mainly middle-class base became apparent: they were hostile and violently aggressive, and most of us didn't know how to cope with it. We provoked this reaction by dancing and kissing close. This brought out their hidden fears about their masculinity, and their reactions included ridicule, throwing beer, and punching — we couldn't start to talk to them. Eventually the manager asked us not to kiss and dance close. Some of us were into going back and confronting them, although the sisters refused to participate. However, as those who were into confrontation didn't know how to react to violence, we stopped going.

Since then we have held a Bizarre,and are having weekly Gay Days in parks in north-west London.We're selling our newssheet regularly to gay pubs, and have just started a coffee stall on the Heath. This is a result of a feeling that we must get out more to the gay community around us — out of our own ghetto.

People started Camden GLF because they found the big Wednesday meetings heavy, aggressive, untogether, and not productive of any personal or strategic results. It seemed to reflect a tension between the old roles of the aggressive politico, and the together love-maker. We decided at the planning meetings in November that the group should be of about a hundred people, splitting up into more local groups as GLF grew in size. We also talked about money, and what our relationship should be with the whole GLF movement. We felt we should be autonomous and as much related to the locality as possible.

We found a meeting-place in Kentish Town, and leafleted

near-by in the shopping streets on Saturdays. This brought quite a number of new people into Camden GLF, although there were many who had been to the bigger Wednesday meetings, and it took some time for everybody to feel a separate Camden identity. Camden seemed to learn from the Wednesday meetings that a leadership structure was to be avoided, so we always broke down into small groups after being together in one big discussion group, then getting together again at the end. We hoped that by doing this, new members would quickly become involved in the meeting, although there was always the problem of reconciling our wish to welcome all gay people whatever views they brought with them, with our need to maintain our own political awareness and to present newcomers with an alternative to the ghetto.

In a big discussion about new premises, some three months after the beginning, the Wednesday meeting syndrome started to re-appear, with votes being taken and clapping after 'speeches'. Everybody, especially the newcomers, was alienated by this heavy atmosphere, so it was decided to try starting the meetings in small groups but getting together into one big discussion at the end. However, without a common topic which would formerly have arisen naturally out of the big general discussion, the small groups lost all sense of urgency, no one liking to impose an arbitrary topic on their group. As a result, enthusiasm and activity dropped; in particular, new people were confused about what was supposed to be going on.

In fact we soon got fed up with inactivity, and after a big rap on legal change, we decided that what we wanted to involve ourselves in was local, not legal action. We began to direct our energy outwards, in the pubs, on Hampstead Heath, and in producing this issue of *Come Together*.

We have had to find out for ourselves how to make our meetings and actions truly collective. The fear of setting up leaders has inhibited our attempts to attack oppression. But in the Camden meetings it has been much easier than it was at the big Wednesday meetings for people to meet each other, make friends and join in the small groups. Perhaps this is because our meetings have been less than a hundred people, mostly living closely to each other in North London. We hope that this will last as we become more active.

Being What Gay Is

The differences between gay people and straight people are important, and maybe we haven't made enough of them in our campaigns against oppression. For one thing, the whole idea of woman relating to woman and man to man shows a positive and good alternative to the way men and women relate to each other. We have within our grasp a chance of more equal relationships with each other than they have. In a society where difference in sex means differences in education, upbringing, clothing, etc. it also means a difference in sexual needs, because emotional and sexual needs are to a large extent caused by the experience of upbringing, education, etc. So a situation exists where we grow up seeing a world which is and always has been run by men, where the word Man means people, where women take on men's names in marriage, where it is said regularly that women's sexual needs are less important and less urgent than those of men. Men are dominant and dominating, and deep down they believe that they are the only important people. So they rule in most situations, and women, in their frustration, with less importance, less weight, less orgasms, less everything, are forced into a role of nagging and bitching to get what they need; and then men say, 'Women run everything, they nag and go on all the time till they get what they want.'

We really are different, and we can be very much more different. As a gay man, I cannot say too much about women relating to each other sexually, because I do not know as much about it as they do, but it seems that they would be aware of each others' emotional and sexual needs — they have the same ones, and they will not be having to relate to someone who thinks they are more important, and who expresses the thought. Also, men relating to men won't be able to impose that trip on each other.

you
CAN
change
yourrole!!

Firstly, the fact that gay men don't want to enter into relationships with women shows that they might have a less inflated idea of their own importance. Whatever it shows, it is certain that it is more easily possible for us to relate equally to each other, because there is no previously decided order as to which member of the couple is superior to the other.

But before this alternative becomes truly possible to us, let alone everyone else, we must recognise the difference between ourselves and straight people, and give it greater importance. The differences between them and us must become us, not just remain inside us. And it is impossible for them to become us when we hide our gayness from most of society. To hide our gayness means to take on the behaviour and roles, clothing and apparent thinking, of straights. Because to conceal being gay does not just involve saying you're straight — it means behaving in such a way as to make people unlikely to think otherwise!

How can we honestly be proud of our gayness and build a gay alternative, when we accept the values that make us unable to tell straight peole that we are gay? If their values are wrong, then only we can make them change, and we can only do that if they can witness what we are. In our society men have privileges that gay men are not always allowed to share in, so some gay men feel tied to the straight life that they are living, in order to hang on to their privileges. But we can only be *free* and *gay* if we can decide to give up the privileges of the people who are in fact the problem. If being gay in our work situations means being thrown out, then maybe that's the break from a life in which we compromise our gayness to suit someone else's wrong values. If we keep the game up, we bludgeon our gayness, be straight to the outside world, and only gay when we are hidden in bed.

It's not enough to say 'I'm a homosexual' and carry on behaving straight. That is not doing anything towards building our alternative, as it is saying that being homosexual doesn't necessarily mean being different from straights, and the alternative we offer can only be built out of the differences. The social behaviour, style, clothes, culture of straight men were devised to bolster up or express the role they play. We cannot behave like them and begin to talk about building equal relationships with each other. Why should the norms that they created imprison us? Coming out means breaking away from that. Coming out means being what gay is. Men whose behaviour and mannerisms are always noticeably gay are the most put down, because they are showing that they don't care about not being proper men, and it is this they're put down for.

Brotherhood

The main problem that we faced in GLF was how difficult the men and women found it to relate to each other. Now that the women have left to get their own thing together, the problem that now confronts us is how can we as men learn to relate properly to each other.

Some of the brothers from Camden got together to talk about this. Obviously, the discussion drew a lot from our own personal experiences. The difficulty that many of us experienced in our relationships was that we still tended to relate in terms of the two roles given us by society. Even though we realise that 'butch' and 'fem' role-playing is a bad thing, as it restricts the total development and expression of our potentialities as people, we still find it too hard to break out of these limiting relationships.

We discovered that we all were troubled by our tendency to separate our minds from our bodies — a way of behaving that everyone in this society is conditioned into. Some of the 'fem' men confessed that while they could open up sexually to 'butch' men, they could only really open up mentally to 'fem' friends, to whom they couldn't relate sexually. They were worried that they were letting themselves be as oppressed as straight women are, by allowing their 'butch' men to make decisions for them. And when they took steps to prevent this happening, they were only opening up less to their lovers. Men who fell into the 'butch' role said that since coming into GLF they had been made aware of how they were oppressing others by their dominating manner. They recognised that they had to become more passive, and of those present all were trying to adopt more 'fem' behaviour.

This led to another problem — with many of the men in various GLF groups trying to be less assertive, too many of us were passive and so not enough was being done. 'Fem' men had to become more assertive (rather than aggressive) in order to counteract this and to develop their personalities. We were all aiming for a happy medium between passivity and assertiveness/ self-confidence.

Because we are all gay men and therefore capable of loving each other, we should find it easier to open up to each other. This is a straight-male-dominated society, straight men have not had their feelings and ways of self-expression challenged as all gay men (especially fem) have. Gay men therefore tend to be more aware, because they have been forced to question themselves and their lives. The 'gay mind' is therefore likely to be more open than the 'straight mind'. (Or should be!) Thus the struggle to relate to each other should be easier for us as gay men than it is for straights.

We do have love on our side, to develop a collective consciousness, and it was obvious from the discussion that we were all anxious to relate honestly and totally to each other, even if we find it difficult at the moment. Collectivism is the only way forward, for while we still cannot cope with each other, we won't be able to cope with and overcome the oppression from straight sexist society. At the same time, we mustn't isolate ourselves from that society by getting into each other so much that we lose contact with the reality of the outside world. But we can only progress in stages. Often, too, we can learn to do this by trying harder to relate to our non-GLF brothers who are still in the ghetto — which will be a way of coping with the necessity of getting through to them. We only have ourselves, and nobody else is going to solve our problems for us.

Midnite on Hampstead Heath

We went to Hampstead Heath at the dead of night to meet our brothers who use the area for cruising. We brought our stove and saucepan and made some coffee and then gave it out to everyone who wanted a drink and a talk. The Heath is used for completely anonymous sex; people cruise each other and have sex, preferably without speaking at all. One of the brothers we spoke to said that was the main attraction of the place. Hunter instincts were aroused and people were there looking specifically for 'animal sex' with no personal complications. He said that the people who were there all went to the pubs and clubs if they wanted more personal contact, and that the Heath was a special place for a special purpose. He said that the police were 'very tolerant' — they only came there to prevent trouble from the queer-bashers. He thought that what we were doing was 'good works', that like all 'do-gooders' we would merely destroy a pattern without providing anything positive to replace it.

Our intention in going to the Heath had been to make contact with people who were too scared to come out, or even to go to the pubs and clubs, and for whom this impersonal anonymous sex was not a free choice, but the only possible outlet for their needs. We had thought we would be able to offer them an alternative to the secrecy and isolation which we had associated with the Heath. If what we had been told was true, then we were in fact being heavy missionaries and by implication putting down and alienating brothers there.

I was worried by this, and also fascinated with the ritual of the place, and I wandered off away from our group and joined in with the cruising in another part of the woods. It was very strange, scary and exciting, a sort of stalking game with a lot of special patterns. I ended up sitting under a tree with someone and we started talking, which was breaking the rules. The reaction this time was very different. We talked about ourselves and other things. He told me that it was the first time he had talked to someone there and he wanted to come to our meetings next week. I found that I had been thinking in terms of us (GLF) and them (cruisers), and then I caught myself in the role of a missionary. Spreading the 'good word' about liberation. It was only when I left our group and started cruising myself that I could stop thinking in terms of categories of 'us and them' and start relating honestly.

I think we should go back there and, providing we don't break up the scene by weight of numbers, but settle away from the main cruising areas and go there individually, we shall be able to add something, without destroying what is already there. We can learn too.

Mike

Awareness

I joined an awareness group because a boyfriend I liked, but somehow found difficult to talk to in the glare of the Wednesday meetings, suggested that I should. I wanted to get to know him, and through him to enter and investigate GLF. Also I wanted to talk about myself to others — people talking about themselves is something which in the straight gay world is more or less forbidden. Conversation with strangers is almost impossible within the 'Do I like him? Does he like me?' syndrome, and conversation with friends and acquaintances is too often inhibited by the secret fear of boring them. Talking to people in the straight gay world reminds me of the way I talk when driving a car. My eyes and mind are on the road.

The others in the group, I found out later, had joined for the same sorts of reasons. We were mostly new to GLF and so could not learn much about it from each other. Instead, with sidelong glances at the Wednesday meetings and the *Manifesto*, we had to re-invent gay liberation for, and by, ourselves.

The random way in which the group was formed, through the office, had the effect of bringing together eleven people who, had they relied on their own social radar, would probably never have met. The fact that we work as a group, that we are able to excite, move, absorb and love each other, is a revelation to some of how constricting and superficial our initial judgements of people often are.

At the moment, after two months of weekly meetings, things are still very pleasant and easy. This worries some of us, who feel that awareness should be tough going most of the time. Despite our confessions and intimate revelations we are still too polite, like strangers on a train, hesitating to hurt as well as simply lacking motive. Confession by itself is too easy. As yet we lack the nerve for confrontation. However, we are beginning to be aware of the ways in which the subliminal ground rules of social intercourse steer us away from pain and embarrassment, and consciously trying to break from those rules.

We recognise that the strongest networks of self-control and self-oppression are the most deeply buried, the ones that it is almost impossible to see, because they are what we see with. Our masculinity and oppression of women are rooted at this level.

At the moment our politeness prevents us from judging each other as a group. Members say what they think of each other, but there is no group view. Yet already the meetings have changed some of us. One of us is giving up his job; another finds, suddenly, paying for sex impossible. The group did not tell them to do these things; it simply provided a context in which these problems could be discussed, thus accelerating the decisions. It is almost like the oracle at Delphi. You come with a question and appear to get no meaningful answer, yet somehow after an evening of rambling conversation and encounter games, the answer is there.

Come Together (Birmingham)14

[*summer 1972*]

Coming Out for 'Straight Gays'

In the words of the GLF *Manifesto*:

> By freeing our heads we get the confidence to come out publicly and proudly as gay people, and to win over our gay brothers and sisters to the ideas of gay liberation.

Confidence is what is needed before we can make any public confession that we are homosexual, and we get that confidence through cutting away at the ideas which have taken root in our minds about the nature of being gay. Our *Manifesto*, however, does not put any emphasis on coming out, but then, neither do most manifestos; the Wittman manifesto mentions it only once, and simply commands, 'come out everywhere'. If there is one thing that gay people wish to avoid at all costs it is making their gay nature part of their reality and part of their public lives.

Before I go further I should make it clear that I have come out — up to a point. I have not come out any more than I have because I am unsure about the importance and emphasis that should be placed on one's sexuality in the context of the rest of one's life. I am speaking, therefore, as an average homosexual who still has some interest, vested or otherwise, in the world that oppresses me. The value of this article is not that it expresses what people at the front of the battlefield think, i.e. that only total coming out is acceptable, but that it expresses what the majority have achieved — self-acceptance, but not total acceptance by those they know outside of the gay world.

When I say that I have some interest in the straight, oppressive world, I mean chiefly that I need some degree of peace and quiet and relative anonymity which only subservience to the status quo can achieve. By accepting a straight role I can sufficiently camouflage my gay nature to free myself from the immediate attacks of the hostile and oppressive society I must live in. Those who reject this society totally also reject the safety of the straight-gay role: they either retire into the depths of the ghetto (an uneasy peace), or they fight it out at the front line. The worst part of that fight is the need for finding self-justification in a mind that is full of thoughts tending, however much below the surface, to assert that our rejection of straight 'reality' is unjustified. The position of the straight gay is that he realises and accepts his gay nature but does not wish to share it with the world any more than the world wishes to share it with him. Straight gay is a compromise of self-acceptance with self-rejection. To put it another way, it is a complicated truce with a world which must remain unavoidably 'outside'.

Is coming out merely admitting that one fancies people of the same sex? That might be the entire depth of one's gayness. Homosexuality is not an absolute condition — it is a relative one where one can be anything from an occasional dabbler in homo-erotic fantasies to an exclusive homosexual who has never had any experience with the opposite sex. In between lies an infinitely fine gradation of bisexuality and confusion. The mistake of many gay people is to imagine that their sex life determines the whole of their lives, from the way they speak to the way they dress and the kind of job they do. I do not accept this argument, though it is one which takes a long time and a lot of careful explanation and deliberation to refute. It would be as well simply to admit, for the sake of this argument, that one's sex life does not determine the whole of one's life but does of course have some effect on it. The question is, how much effect?

Those who maintain that sex determines most of what we are also see coming out as a big thing, involving change of lifestyles and a revolution in the kind of values we hold. It is akin to the Christian viewpoint that accepting Christ changes our life, making us 'new creatures', 'born again'. The difference between the rebirth of the Christian faith and the rebirth of the gay faith is that the former is convened by a supernatural agent. Is gay power a supernatural force capable of infusing us with a mind-changing power from outside? The change wrought in some of the religious gay liberationists is not supernatural, but an unconscious and workable analysis of what self-oppression is and what is needed to counteract it. The motivation comes from inside them.

The average straight gay is not so motivated. For him or her the rebirth approach to coming out is not possible, because they are adjusted to straight reality sufficiently well not to have any desire to endure the labour pains of any rebirth. This is where I stand; as I said, my coming out has not progressed to the point where I feel that much different to what I felt before I made it a feature of my public life that my sexual orientation was different to those I work or play with. The only difference I can detect is that I am no longer consciously or intentionally 'oppressive' to other males or to women. My attitude to others is that they are equals, in contrast to some of my fellow males who look upon women and gay people as inferior. In being what I am not, I feel that I have achieved enough coming out, and that to go any further would be reactionary and an unreasonable advance into something that is not naturally 'me'.

It is important that we avoid the same stereotype role-playing that we are trying to avoid; what I mean is that we do not stop being 'male' only to become 'female', if that is not what we are. There is a tendency for some gay people to feel that their reality is so real that it must be a standard for all other gay people. This is what the straight oppressors think, and we are trying to avoid their mistake.

So far I have been able to use words like 'straight' and 'gay' uncritically, but now is the time to reject them, at least in what they imply. We are gay people — but some are more gay than others. Gay is a stereotype which the non-homosexual, male-chauvinist world has caused by its rejection of homosexuality. The 'queen' of the old world, so effectively and revoltingly portrayed by such comedians as Kenneth Williams, or the drag queens of the London clubs, is not a lifestyle which gay people have developed 'naturally'; it is a reaction, an obsession with a stereotype which they adopt in order to avoid the impossible stereotype of the 'straight' male. Coming out, therefore, does not imply the adoption of the 'queen' stereotype or any other form of role-play (like the pseudo-hippy or freak persona), just so we can give ourselves a slap in the face, in the hope that we will also be slapping society. Coming out should imply the discovery of our real selves, but that, I hasten to add, is not something which will happen overnight, if it is capable of happening at all.

What I am attempting to show is that there is a lot more to real coming out than merely admitting publicly that we are homosexuals. We cannot admit to anything, without deluding ourselves, unless we are sure that it is true. We know we like having sex with others of our own sex, but what we do not know is where sex ends and the natural terrain of life begins. Freud, beware, has haunted us with the ghost of his theories more than we care to realise. Those who aspire to seeing into themselves had better know something about Freudian ideology, or they will not be able to avoid seeing themselves through a very distorted glass. Freudian psychology is merely the scientific expression of the sexism which has existed in our society for hundreds of years. Freud discovered nothing; he merely gave an old oppression a new force.

In conclusion, I have come out where my homosexuality is concerned; I admit to liking men, but not to anything else. In doing this I have had to accept myself and be sure that it is up to me to decide where my sexual inclinations lie. I see no more honour in liking men than women, and whatever privileges may accrue from using women as sex objects, they are not the kind of privileges I wish to accept. I cannot, at this point in my life, see any other sort of oppression or secret desire in myself that I might possibly want to come out over. I play a 'straight' role in a 'straight' society because it satisfies my want of relative calm. I do not feel obliged to play that role, and I know that I can change my role whenever I feel like it, providing that I am prepared to make the requisite sacrifice. This attitude, however, is a compromising one, however honest it might appear to be. It is the attitude of the many gay people, inside and outside of GLF, who still cling to some small part of the 'outside' world, and it is what the total gay liberationists hotly reject. But the choice between 'total' liberation and sexual liberation is not an easy one to make — it is difficult, even, to see that it does in fact exist. Sartre's dictum that we are 'condemned to be free' is where I begin, and where I end is at Rousseau's idea that 'man is born free and everywhere he is in chains'.

Trevor

Coming Out as a Transsexual

I have, in the last twelve months, 'come out' as a transsexual and I can truly say that I have never been happier. Further and ultimate happiness for me lies somewhere in the far distant future, but it is a goal to aim for.

At the time of my coming out I had never heard of GLF or its aims and ambitions, so my coming out was possibly much more of a personal ideology than for our brothers and sisters who have attended a number of GLF meetings and been helped by them to obtain true happiness.

Possibly, involving coming out as a transsexual is much more than just wearing a badge and telling anybody who asks about the badge to explain that you are gay and attempting to have them realise what you mean and accepting that you are 'different' from them.

Unlike most other brothers and sisters, my coming out was prompted by police action, after being taken to court for 'conduct likely to cause a breach of the peace' (not 'piece'). After this experience I retreated even further into my shell and was so disillusioned by the publicity I received I attempted one of the age-old methods to finish it all. Happily I am glad to say I failed, otherwise I would not have found the happiness I now have.

After a few months of living as a hermit I contacted the Samaritans, and after a few meetings with them I was able to talk about myself, my aims and ambitions, and finally reached a complete understanding with myself.

Once I had admitted my true inner self to others I felt great relief (this I take to be one of the main aims of GLF), and thereupon decided to be myself all the time and live life as it suited me and not the way I had been committed to live since coming out of the womb.

Prior to this, my marriage (to a woman) had broken up and my wife was seeking a divorce together with the custody of the children because of my attitude to life, namely brought about because of my jealousy of her femininity and her ability to become pregnant and know true happiness within the straight society.

Once I had decided to come out I did so. The last time I wore male clothing was the day after I had made my decision, when I was so apprehensive that I had to go to the local paper shop to buy cigarettes at 6.30 in the morning (ugh! what a time to go out). Since then I only wear female clothing and now I wonder how I ever wore such constricting clothing as trousers and male clothing in general, as there is not so much scope within that framework to express your individuality fully.

Since coming out I have been ostracised completely by my former friends and neighbours, I have been harassed on many occasions by the police but now they have spoken to me on a number of occasions and they seem to realise that if we are to get along together their attitude must change as I most certainly will never return to their ideas of straight society.

I live in a small town (200,000), just north of Birmingham, and consequently I am known to a great many people who knew me 'before'. I imagine, by the way they laugh, sneer, and jeer at me that they are embarrassed by me, but I have not yet found out if this is because they will not admit their own inhibitions to themselves.

Since joining GLF and getting one of their badges, I feel happier again as I realise the numbers of gay people in GLF and outside it (unhappily at the moment) understand and accept me as a person, and not a pair of trousers or a dummy in a shop window wearing whatever clothes society in general dictates that I should be attired in at any given moment. Wearing the GLF badge is like a shield to me and it feels as if it is protecting me, although now that I have accepted and revel in my femininity, I now have to be liberated again as in many ways I have accepted the sufferance of women and lack of liberty afforded to them by the male-orientated society. For instance, I feel wrong in smoking in the street or going into a pub on my own, but I don't suppose I can hope for complete miracles to happen in such a short time and will have to work hard at my accepted role in life.

Julia

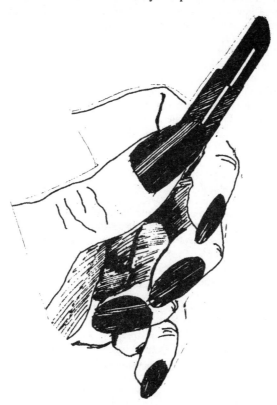

Come Together (Notting Hill) 15

[*spring 1973*]

Happy Families

This issue of *Come Together* has been written and laid out by Notting Hill GLF. Nearly all the people who contributed to it have lived here at some time or other recently, whether in the commune which has come to rest here, or outside it.

Since most of the magazine has been conceived in the Notting Hill commune (there's also one at Muswell Hill), here's some facts about the origins and history of the group.

The original group started in Brixton, where they managed to get a house big and cheap enough, which is really difficult when all the agents can see you are gay.

There were eight of us then. We had a great time going out in drag and make-up — we were all drawing from the confidence that living together gave us. Very soon the boys at the comprehensive school across the road got to hear (or see) about us, and it became the morning pastime to toss bricks through our front-room window. Talking to them didn't help much, especially later when the inspector told us that we would get done for importuning if we invited any more of them into the house.

It seemed to me that the first thing to do was to establish some sort of basic terms for us to at least get through that we were no longer a passive target for student oppression. The alarm was sounded, and for two or three days the house at Brixton was filled with the heavier element of those caring about GLF. We sat up all night after the first wave of attack, and in the morning decided to draft a leaflet to give out to the students at the school. This was to make clear two things: that we were not going to sit still and be pummelled into the ground by *anyone*, and that there were plenty more where we came from. Also the pamphlet explained a bit about who we were and what we were trying to do. Well, the next day we marched into the school in full paint and drag of various kinds and did our thing. We were of course chucked out by the pigs, and no one on the staff wanted to talk.

It became very clear that the commune as such could no longer go on growing in such an atmosphere of violence and poisonous vindictiveness, so it was decided to leave the stonier ground of Brixton and on to the slightly less stony area of Notting Hill Gate. Here at least was the appearance of comparative peace. But by no means your verdant pastures! It is an area, as we all know, which has got itself a reputation for having an (albeit questionable) vaguely community awareness — where people are known to have at least listened to one another's grievances. But let no one think it's in any way a haven of rest, particularly for gays.

There was a house vacant in cosy Colvillia which miraculously opened its doors to the brothers from Brixton. They were, on a certain level, surrounded by friends, who they knew would support them in the event of trouble. As it turned out, the main trouble came when the Notting Hill Housing Trust were not as helpful at first as they have now promised they will be, and street violence broke out when they tried to evict us without the appropriate court order. Well, the ever hungry press men arrived, and as a result the Trust were embarrassed into behaving themselves in a slightly more humane manner, and are now at the point where they have told us that they will consider seriously a two to three-year term house for us — we'll see won't we? Meanwhile, the people in the commune are different people from those who originally came from Brixton, but the mind-blowing concept of true communal living remains intact, and seems to get stronger every day. So here we are — come up and see us sometime. We are squatting in a disused film studio with no bath but plenty of bubbles. See you soon, and take care.

Many but not all of us have been active in GLF since the beginning. We didn't know each other then, but through involvement we got to know each other as friends whilst still living within the framework of our particular flats (territory). One other artificiality was that we related to each other as friends whilst being aware of the growing love that existed betweeen us.

Coming into the commune and sharing everything, our material possessions of course, our ideas, our energy, our minds and our bodies, meant that we had to change ourselves from being friends to being lovers. The best way of describing it is for you to imagine making it with your best friend, the one you call 'sister', and remove the taboo of incest from exploring sexually. You know you love your best friends, but expressing and exploring that love physically! It is not important, you say, but what is more important than love? Making money, perhaps? Or is it the size of your cock and the size of his cock that's at the bottom of it?

You never really know another person until you live with them. The question is, how much do you want to know? How much are you prepared to show? What are you afraid of hiding?

We find we cannot accept the old red herring of not 'fancying' each other, which avoids the issue, and in reality is a put-down of placing others in a stereotype role, butch, bitch or whatever, and failing to see the uniqueness and beauty behind that projected facade. Were we to go on behaving only in terms of cocks and bums and 'de rigeur', obligatory, orgasms, or to try and work that one out, and just turn on and melt into each others' bodies?

Friends, to outsiders, appear solid, but inside, one competes with the other — keeping up with the Jones's! Lovers cannot compete without oppressing one another and denying that love. Even touching each other to begin with was difficult — try stroking your 'sister' and see in his eyes and the tenseness of his body the internal alarm signal, trying to work out why.

We can only begin with what we've got, and where it doesn't fit, struggle for change. Solidarity doesn't come with visions from thin air, it is to do with you and me, expanded, multiplied and distributed equally amongst us all. It is to do with love, because without love there can be no change and nothing to support that change. Without love there is only games and competition and distrust, and to believe that love and loving relationships are not fundamental to solidarity is to fool oneself with intellectual games.

The trust some of us felt for each other as friends prior to coming into the commune, and the trust we tried to build with the others we didn't know, helped us to realise that our former friendships, in this example between three people all mutually reinforcing each other, were in a larger communal situation a barrier creating an us and a them. B knew his own feelings for A, and A's sexual attraction, but couldn't get that together. Saw from C's behaviour that C felt the same way about A, but didn't discuss the situation with C at all. B and C were friends. C and B were friends, but C only saw A and never thought that B was involved. A wasn't conscious of B and C's feelings, as he didn't feel sexually attracted to them. What had been built up was a pyramid with A at the top, B and C next, competing with each other while keeping the rest below and controlling their approaches to A. Sexual guilt had built a hierarchical structure in the minds of at least two of us, and in spite of our awareness it was shocking to discover how dishonest we had been, with ourselves and each other, in what seemed to us at that time a close relationship. The experience showed us once again that monogamous relationships did not work, just as they have not done for any of us in the past.

All of us are uniquely different in the ways we have been oppressed, have had these 'special relationships' and have had to work through them in order to find ourselves and each other through nine pairs of eyes. The younger of us have felt oppressed by the older ones and their adult tricks, which maintained their 'control' over others. Tricks acquired in order to attain or maintain some shitty middle-class view of themselves as experienced men. This was another division into them and us. How do we begin to relate to people younger than us with a clearer picture of what it's all about, without destroying that vision and clarity beneath attitudes acquired out of trying to live for up to twenty years within society? The precise age range here is 17 to 37, and the question that forms is who don't we turn to when we need help in understanding something, and why? Do we teach our children, or do they teach us? Does life run forwards or backwards?

What it comes down to is feeling, and being honest with each other about one's feelings, all the time and in every living situation we encounter. Why do I feel like this? What do others feel? Can we feel together?

One danger we feel is in rationalising our emotions, because we find as soon as that happens it stifles the emotion completely, we lose the power to be honest at that moment, and the intellect waves its spiny male intellectualisation over everything. We know a lot of this paper appears intellectual to many people, and a very real barrier to communication, but what can we really say, except that many of the things we feel are sometimes difficult to put into words? Describing our reality and our love is hard to put into words. We really feel we can only live it, but the catch is, no one allows us to, not even in the gay ghetto when we pop on a frock and pop out. We reject your fantasies of who we are, just as we reject the previous images of what we once were or chose to be, now that we no longer relate to them.

Class division showed itself clearly here, in the way possessions, work and people were treated. Working class; middle class. Working class trying to prove as good as (competing with) the middle class. We have felt that oppression and traced those divisions back in our memories, and discovered for instance how the middle classes drive all feelings out of their children by the age of seven, leaving them alone with an intellect which grows to distrust the feelings: need we say, of themselves, of others . . . masses! . . . paranoia!!

Awareness is not just an intellectual diversion on Friday nights, it requires every ounce of feeling there is for every minute of every month, year of life.

We have found two marvellous ways of opening up to our senses and keeping in touch with our feelings. The more we learn about each other in the commune, the higher we get: much higher than anything that came after flower power. Yes, we too once threw our hands up in horror at all the images of flying out of windows, dirt, disease and wasting away. Those images were thrown out by the so-called underground or alternative society when applying their weedy political liberalism, leapt on gleefully by Fleet Street, to titillate people bored by war, more war, civil war, murder and rape.

When you think of the male 'drop-outs', whatever that might mean, all you see is beads and hair, drab and dreary stereotype clothing (American roadies), their brown rice grot, dressed up as magic and the mystery of macrobiotic. You see a middle-class hype, and the underground is as much of a mess as straight society; with no direction to go.

Flower power brought with it things to change the consciousness of people, but the underground that developed out of that, the freak, the cat, the head, could only drop out. Being men, with no reason to change themselves as individuals in the ways they think and relate to the world around them, they end up by continually beating their brick heads against the walls of their own male chauvinism. Nothing grows on the underground but dreams of the past and disillusionment.

Nevertheless, flower power still offers an opportunity to experience a higher consciousness and all the beauty of life, and we know how to use it. Gay people are not frightened of change, of being different, in the way men are. We can be camp, we can express ourselves in ways men wouldn't dare to, being so straight and conformist. Even behind closed doors men behave the same (and we know that!), out of fear of being thought different.

You know what alcohol does to people, it makes them stupid and very aggressive, it is in fact a depressant, fine for making people accept a dreary monotonous routine. A man's drink!

We turn on to ourselves for the way it brings us together, for the calm reflection that it brings and the sometimes giggly high. We can allow ourselves to be wafted warmly to a position where problems can be looked at from different angles. It clears the head, gets you high and gives you the energy to think. We get from it the delicacy of feeling, a clarity of vision, the perception of oneself and other beings that cannot be imagined over a gin and tonic. And of course the colours, and we've never known a queen who hadn't an eye for colour. Above all, the sheer enjoyment it brings has helped us all enormously to overcome blocks in our personal relationships; those oppressive fuck-ups which prevent us from sharing all we have. It teaches us also from past experiences that there is much more we want to know, and there are still many questions which we haven't as yet even begun to formulate.

War-Baby Working-Class Gay

I was born in June 1941. A war baby. I have never known my father — he seems to have mysteriously disappeared soon after my birth. My two sisters and I were brought up by our mother, who went out charring in order that we all might eat and be clothed.

Practically the whole city had been razed to the ground, but the rich still managed to live well, amongst all the suffering and destruction. There was a very smart restaurant called Genoni's, where all the privileged were still able to eat their steaks and drink their wines, while the rest of the population barely existed above starvation level. It was this place that my mother arrived at at six every morning, to clean and hoover after the previous night's revels. My earliest experience was of sitting on a table at three years old whilst my mum pulled one of the great red velvet divans from the wall amd jumped on it, and rats ran out of the upholstery to be caught again by the cats and dogs while I screamed my lungs out in terror.

We were bombed out three times, but eventually mum was able to rent a three-storey house with semi-basement, on Plymouth Hoe. This house was situated on the boundary of the Hoe, which was supposed to be 'chic and smart', and the Barbican, which was the harbour area where the fishing families lived in total slum conditions and surrounded on all sides by bombed-out houses. As kids we had a ball, with the bomb sites as our playground in the winter and the Hoe and the beach in the summer. We were a total community of children, who hadn't a care in the world and had quite friendly relations (most of the time) with the other street gangs near us. We were in no way aware of our poverty as we had no yardstick by which we could measure our conditions, we all went to either the local Catholic or C of E primaries, and all the kids were from similar backgrounds.

The concept of wealth gradually became apparent through our education. We were being made aware ever so subtly of our parents' lowly status through the process of education. Not only were we made aware of it, but also made to feel ashamed of it as well. Just to take the edge off our guilt about being poor, we were encouraged to collect pennies for the 'poor black babies' who were worse off than ourselves, or so we were told. (Where were the seeds of racism being sowed?) This, together with all the stories of how things were much better before the war and food was much more plentiful, you didn't need ration books, and sweets were to be found in abundance. Slowly, slowly the seeds of discontent were begining to take root. The beginnings of the 'divide and rule' policies of the ruling minority were beginning to manifest themselves among the gang.

We were beginning to compare status with the rest of the kids, and the gang started to break into various 'class groups' with the very poor right at the bottom to be shat on by all the others.

Mum became dissatisfied with the 'education' at our local Catholic school, because it was rumoured that they had a low 11-plus record of passes. My elder sister had failed and had to go to a secondary modern; I, being the only son upon whom all hopes were pinned, had to be placed in a school that had a 'good record'. We were all sent to school in Devonport, out of our area and meeting new kids for the first time. Class consciousness was rife, we were ridiculed because we came from the Barbican, and were called a load of scruffs.

We had to defend ourselves, and the only non-violent way was to lie and exaggerate our situation. The fact that we thought our father had been killed in the war was a great help. We played that one for all the pity we could milk from it. I failed twice to get an A pass in my 11-plus, but due to a lot of behind-the-scenes manipulating by the nuns on behalf of my mum, I was able to get into the only Catholic grammar school.

From the age of seven right up to my going to grammar school at twelve, my sex life was very constant in its frequency and pleasure. There were at least five other boys in the gang who used to get it on with each other, either in pairs or all together. A boy called Russ and I were lovers for three years. He was the leader of the gang and was everything I was not, big, beautiful and strong. His parents owned two shops down the road, so he was in fact middle-class and the leader in every sense of the word. He was two years older than me, and when he failed to get into grammar school his parents gave him hell. We were still lovers right up to the day he first saw me in my new school uniform. He saw me coming across the bomb site, and attacked me with a knife. God alone knows what shit his parents had been throwing at him to freak him out so much, but I have hardly seen him since that day.

Grammar school was full of middle-class and upper-middle-class boys, with heads to match. My mother had at the same time been keeping abreast with my progress by turning the house into a lodging-house for the labourers and craftsmen who were pouring in to rebuild the city. She was at a later date able to leave her working-class background completely behind, by graduating from taking in lodgers to summer visitors. She had become a respectable middle-class seaside landlady. The whole of my grammar-school education was geared to university and/or priesthood. Religion was rammed down our throats, it was like force-feeding geese ready for the delicatessen counter. There was, not very far from the surface, something within me which kept telling me that the whole scene was a load of shit. Something which surfaced on the odd occasion, but at most times had to be kept under control as they tried to blind me with facts and figures and cripple my freedom with religion. During my five years at the grammar school I did not have a single sexual encounter, although at various times I fell in love with an art master and a form master. I left at the age of seventeen, after failing most of my O-levels. I couldn't stand another year of religion and prison. I came to London (to see the Queen!) six months later, and got a job as a junior window-dresser at Debenham and Freebody's.

I was working daily with some of the most expensive and 'luxurious' clothes in the world. After a few months in London my sexuality was reawakened by finding the key to the gate of the gay closet. I stepped smartly in; at last I was beginning to feel more comfortable about my surroundings and friends. I very soon became aware that a Devonshire accent and late-fifties working-class fashions were a passport to oblivion. So faced were many of my gay contemporaries, with a completely new lifestyle. I had a choice to make: either accept the values of the closet or get out. I accepted the closet; if nothing else I could at least be alone with others like me.

People were not interested in me as a personality, only as a body. I was never aware of my own attraction, cause all my life I had worn glasses and been oppressed for it, so I could never be really sure why people went to bed with me. I realise now it was probably just youth and a decent-sized cock. Having slipped into the gay closet, I tried and fooled myself for many years that I had succeeded in losing the accent and natural camp. It horrifies me to think how totally unaware I was of myself and others around me. How can anybody who has been conditioned into deceit and dishonesty ever hope to be truthful?

I rose from junior to managerial status during the next twelve years, but became unhappy and ill. During my straight-gay life I experienced most material 'rewards'. I started my life by being born into poverty, and my gay life by being poor. I stopped working for others soon after I nearly had my second breakdown. I started to live on my wits, and digging experiences as they happened. Funnily enough it took me twelve years to finally cut through all the guilt and conditioning, before I took to the streets at the age of 29 as a whore. My fear overrode my poverty at 17, so many times I went hungry; by the time I was 29 my experience had enabled me to cut through all the shit and rules and regulations, and look at the world and society from a more honest viewpoint. Honest not because what I was doing was right, but because I'd always secretly wanted to do it but never had the courage. I was beginning to acknowledge myself and my desires, and not buckle down to the image of what people wanted me to be. I was beginning to follow intuition and instinct, as opposed to logic and reason.

Two years ago I joined GLF, and ever since the first moment I have known that I was for the first time in my life doing what I wanted to do. GLF is a key and only a key through which gay people can begin to understand their oppression right the way through back to the beginning. I have now and am still being confronted with all the insidious ways in which this sick society operates, and how I as a gay male have contributed to the sickness by my own guilts, fears and prejudices. Behind me now I hope is the falseness of the material values. I am at this moment back to square one, living in poverty with twelve beautiful brothers, having to collect water from next door because society fears the solidarity of gay people. They want to crush us, and all that we are striving for, and they intend to use every method at their disposal. Divide and rule amongst the gays is easy to operate, because hetero men make the rules, and up to now anything that has been known about homosexuality has been written by men with a definite vested interest in keeping the status quo. The biggest visible stranglehold the ruling minority has over gays is guilt and fear about their sexuality. Couple this with the material rewards system, and a whole lot of other equally dangerous but far more suitable controls, and the circle becomes almost impossible to break.

The material drawbacks in trying to live a new lifestyle are as many as they are complex, and I think it is fear of losing the so-called material securities which holds many gays back from coming out. The worst possible loss for a good many gays is a loss of face and status. The sooner gays really start to look into the status quo and suss out the lies and falseness, the better. It is not the radical drag which is freaking most gays, as is generally put about, but the loss of material status.

Getting Down to the Nitty-Gritty

Two years since GLF was started here. Two years since sexual liberation has changed from being a political tactic to the hard realisation that this is the only way any revolutionary ideas proposed by women or gay people (or others) can be honestly considered without them being mere facades for male ego-trippers.

In GLF itself, this time has been spent in a variety of explorations and diversions into the generalisations of the ideas proposed in the *Manifesto*. Sexism began life as a word; it obscured realities we were not then aware of. It is now, for myself at least, a harsh reality that *every* man in the world benefits from: *gay* men pour shit on *all* women as well as straight men. For others it was and is a reality, but they have touched on it and retreated into their own male pride.

Sexism is not just a word but the expression of the fact that over half of the world (women) are oppressed by the rest (men) and the consequent fucking mess we live in.

Most of GLF talked of the *Manifesto* as if it were an engraved stone tablet; but possibly GLF's most important achievement was to break down the personal (ego?) barriers between a few people, who actually, through a closer rapport and support than could ever be achieved outside GLF, began to investigate sexual liberation as outlined in the *Manifesto* — with particular reference to themselves. They began to *do* what they *said*. Those who did not do as they said were seen for what they were — hollow political mouthpieces.

There were many ways in the *Manifesto* through which people could explore and change themselves: some gay women realised that gay men were as oppressive as other groups of oppressed men, and split to work away from men. A commune was set up, which eventually began to relate the passage in the *Manifesto* on destroying the family unit by experimenting in communal living. (This copy of *Come Together* was produced by a second gay male commune that came into being in June 1972.) Some gay men began to explore the media in an alternative way. But all the experiments done by gay men were done as men first and gay second. Gradually, as this was realised — not in the obvious way, but simply because many ideas did not achieve anything — they were dropped. They could go no further without destroying their male privilege. What they were trying to do was opposed to male domination, so obviously they could not proceed if they were still dominating males.

Male Privilege

This led to the limbo that GLF found itself in last summer, and which continued into this year. There was then a polarisation of activity.

Gay men who decided they would not attempt to destroy their male privilege, their sexism, the root of their oppression and oppressiveness, began to renew activity on another front, that of liberal gay politics; *Gay News*, with all its journalistic hypocrisy and hollow words, was the first blunder in this direction. The newly formed Gay Civil Rights group, simply by using that name, is another.

Other gay men saw that if the *Manifesto* and their commitment to GLF had any honesty and truth, then they had to explore ways of destroying their male-derived privileges. They saw that it was only in this way that they could begin to relate honestly as individuals to both women and men, and not as stereotypes of oppression. They saw that this was, for them, the only true alternative way of furthering any truly revolutionary ideas, and that in itself it was revolutionary. They saw that without doing this, all their previous ideas and actions were token. They are into understanding their oppression and self-oppression, and their oppressiveness, and creating change in themselves through greater awareness of themselves in society (i.e. how they support it and how they can destroy it).

Drag and the Male and Female Myth

They wear clothes that society only permits women to wear. This is the ultimate external rejection of the male role in society, and as such, all queens (men who wear make-up and dresses) are rejected by society because they destroy the myth about men. Ultimately, all men are jealous of women, which is why they have come to dominate them and destroy their freedom, and any man who admits this threatens society's stability.

'Jealousy of women' is a difficult idea to appreciate, as one's usual definition of women is one provided by a male-dominated society; men have created a myth about women. The creation of this myth began when male aggressiveness was used against female creativity and harmony. Aggression now has no place in society, when it might have done in the past, for there is no need to procreate in a contrived security, and no need to kill for food. Male aggression is the root of all society's ills, for if it did not exist, the money and labour, machines and energy used in its maintenance could easily be channelled into creating an equal society; but this would be a society where men as we know them would have no place, so men strive for the continuation of the female myth.

By wearing drag, I feel that I am helping to destroy the male myth as well as the female myth. I enjoy, when wearing a dress, many of the traits that men used to be allowed to enjoy, but which are now buried under the male myth. Make-up, when used as a way of putting women down, is effective as it creates objects of them — mere beautified possessions; but when used by men, it turns this on its head by re-applying it to men: it is a demonstration, in society's terms, of a man externalising his femininity.

This helps me to destroy my aggressiveness, by isolating it as a negative factor in myself, a barrier between me and love for other men and women. I destroy it by living in a way in which it has no place (obviously difficult in an aggression-ridden society) — a communal way.

Communal Living

In a commune, survival and attention should not have to be fought for; the first is supplied by living together, and the second is unnecessary — a male way of supporting one's ego.

For me, drag has been a way in which I have met other people who were into the same thing. It has been a source of strength for attempting communal living and communal work, new ways of relating and new ways of thinking.

When I initially had an opportunity of joining the commune that I at present live in, I did not do so for several reasons. I felt that I would not be able to continue painting, an occupation which had helped me survive an all-male schooling, by isolating me from the other men. I felt also that I would like to join a group with more people in it that I knew. Now, after living in a commune for two months, I can see that what I was looking for in the commune was a position of greater security from which I could attack my male ego. This could not be done as an isolated individual. I only joined when those people who I wanted to live with had also joined. I knew that I would be more secure in the commune. I knew that it was the only place where I could live the way I wanted to live — or rather where I didn't have to live the way society wanted me to live. It was the only place where freedom could exist for me. I now no longer am able to shut myself off from people as this occupation would have me do; I was now able to use the thought and creativity that had been employed in this way, towards constructing the commune with my other gay brothers.

There are many problems that arise when ten gay men live together in one room as we are at present. There are the problems about who does the shit-work that men usually force women to do, such as washing, cooking and cleaning. There are problems about who works and how we sort out the money differences in the commune. There are problems about tidiness, music, sex and many other things.

The only way any of these problems have been overcome or tackled is because we are at last able to love each other in a non-competitive, truly honest way. It is the energy arising from this love that has bound us together and contained the internal explosions that have occurred.

Sex and Orgasm

The most complicated raps we have had have been about sex, or rather what it meant to us, and our sexual relationships within and outside the commune. My idea that an orgasm constitutes sex has been destroyed, because I have got more pleasure out of other forms of emotional communication, such as kissing or experiencing the body or bodies of one's lovers. I still find having an orgasm incredibly pleasurable, but the sucking or fucking or mutual masturbation that leads up to an orgasm often are the result of male ego-games that are employed to play a role — whether it is one of domination or submission. I do not doubt that sex orgasm is possible without these games, but it requires, I feel for myself, an experiencing of other non-defined forms of love making.

Communication

One of the problems I have encountered in writing this article has been in expressing myself in a way that communal living, and attempting to create an alternative, are not conducive to. Living in a commune has encouraged me to a less easily readable, in society's terms, way of expression. My ideas do not flow in the old reasoned logical arguments, but are rather ideas that spread like oil on drops of water, at first concentrated and later more diffuse. I am expressing experiences that society has banned, and so the language has been also suppresed, or rather, never invented.

In conclusion, I would like to say that the reason why I feel so strongly about drag is that it has enabled me to achieve what I have at the moment. I know that society as we know it must be destroyed. I know that it must be destroyed because it is dominated by men for their benefit only, with the consequent destruction of women; this has meant that no one is able to *live*. If I am to help in the destruction of society, I, as a gay man, must not support society by conforming to its male myth: I must help destroy this myth, and the female myth. Wearing drag has been my stepping-off point for destroying my own male myth and helping other people in destroying theirs. Until this is done, I cannot, I feel, contribute validly to the feminist revolution that women's liberation are engaged in at present, and I feel that this is the only way, at present, open to us to change the world.

All you MEN Come Out and Do It!

One thing I think I now see clearly. That is that those gay men who attack queens so vigorously are the ones who most want to get into drag, the ones who are most threatened by it. I would like to say to them, *do it!* Drag subverted my male myth, perhaps it will do that to yours.

Of Queens and Men

I am sick and tired of going to GLF meetings, discos, dances, etc. and being seized upon and attacked as a 'radical feminist': it seems that people cannot see me as an individual, purely, it seems, because of the way I dress. Surely this in itself says a lot for prejudice in GLF. Nobody has ever explained to me what a radical feminist man is, what this term, so freely thrown about, actually means. As far as I can make out, radical feminists are women; I myself am a man. When thrown at me it is fairly obvious that the term is not exactly complimentary, and thus it is a put-down for radical feminist women, and therefore all women. Whenever I ask the men concerned what it means, they usually react with a 'don't give me any of that' and vague none-too-audible mutterings of 'fascists in frocks telling us what to do'. I explain that I've never met the man before, and am certainly not interested in what he does, so long as his behaviour is not oppressive to others, including myself. After all, revolution is about fighting oppression on all levels, within and without. The inevitable reply is the 'I'm-not-oppressing-you-you're-oppressing-us' routine, which continues, in reply to my startled eyebrows, with the 'we were quite happy until you started coming here wearing dresses and make-up'. 'The whole way you walk in with a group of your friends is condescending.'

Perhaps we do seem like that when we arrive, but at the same time we usually arrive together because we live together. I stop myself from asking the man in question if perhaps we should each have a car to drive on our own so that we can arrive intermittently. And how many men in GLF have ever been on public transport in drag? Well, to put it mildly, it helps to have a friend or two, and to make a joke of the whole scene. We *are* defensive when we walk in, just as, as a young Jewish boy, I used to feel defensive walking into a room where I knew the people inside, or some of them, were definitely prejudiced. And I know that when I go into a GLF meeting, nine times out of ten I'm going to get a hostile reaction. I know that at least half the people in the room think of me in terms of all the wild rumours and myths that have been spread by individual power-hungry men within GLF, their commercial gay press (or would-be commercial gay press) which is devoted to dividing and destroying GLF, a slight case of vengeance lust — we wouldn't let them get to the top in their man-games; the underground press whom we wouldn't let rule us; the straight press. And all these have played on the prejudice against feminine men that somewhere has been instilled in us all.

I suppose that I have learnt to ignore all this, learnt, for my own protection, not to let it upset me, and ignore the people who react to me in this way. It is this that frightens me; I want to talk to them, to explain where I am at, but their prejudices categorise me. Can they not see that this is no way; that they are being manipulated; that the only way we can get anywhere is by listening to what each other has to say, rather than scoring a win over the next one?

But there is another reaction I get, related but different. It contains the same prejudice and contempt, but is far more obviously indicative of that bogey, the male ego. I get my bottom pinched; I get told that I have good legs. Sure they're good, they walk and kick out the odd chorus line and generally do what's required of them. These men think that because I wear a frock I want to be treated as an oppressed woman, that I want the oppressive criteria applied to women applied to myself; in other words I'm just longing to be oppressed. Well I'm not; the wank is over. And when I'm not delighted at the 'compliment', I am being condescending (they tell me). Why do so many men in GLF think that because I am a queen I am longing for their prick, that I cannot resist them, that they are indispensable to my happiness? Why are they so put out when I tell them that I do not want them on those terms, that I do not crave them for their maleness, that I do not 'want' anybody? I only want to share, to love, and it cannot be done where criteria are used to 'evaluate' someone's desirability. (But I've heard all this before — that's why I came into GLF — to fight that oppression and at the same time to escape the oppression of the straight world; and straight doesn't to me refer to sexual preferences.)

To me, being a queen means ridding myself of thinking between the legs, of thinking in terms of being turned on by being dominated or dominating, of thinking of a prick as something particularly desirable. It's only another wrinkled little bit of flesh after all.

I am a queen because I choose to be a queen; because all things that are esteemed as male or butch are oppressive in that they put down the feminine, and thus women. Our oppression as gay men has the same root as all oppression, as the oppression of women, as the oppression of any one group by another. The root is the cult of the man, the cult of competition, the cult of aggression. It is this that makes the father the ruler of the family; it is this that makes one man wish to be at the top, the hierarchical basis of our society, the hierarchical basis of oppression. One group (and the first group delineation is, of course, gender) desires to be more powerful than the next, and within each group each man desires to be at the top.

It is all this that the term Man implies to me — this is why I find men's clothing repulsive and totally lacking in beauty, and this is why I find men who cultivate being men repulsive — and as long as they are not prepared to examine how they oppress others they are my enemies; but if we could help each other to examine our own oppressiveness, it could be beautiful.

To me revolution is change, continuous change — this is the only way we can begin to grow.

Come Together (Manchester) 16

[*summer 1973*]

Don Milligan:
'The Politics of Homosexuality'

This pamphlet was written primarily as an attempt to get gay politics discussed among the International Socialists. Don is a member of that group, as well as belonging to Lancaster GLF. As such the pamphlet does not add much to the statement of our oppression in the London GLF *Manifesto*, but the political programme he proposes is different, and it is this I would like to discuss.

Don argues that there are two main reasons for our oppression — one, that we undermine the family and marriage, and two, that we, particularly the butch dyke and the screaming queen, make a mockery of the roles women and men are supposed to play. The role of the family in repressing children and training them for their future roles, ties in fairly clearly with the need of the capitalist system for a particular kind of worker and for the repression of sexuality. (Don says countries such as Cuba and the USSR have been no less oppressive to gay people.) But the connection between capitalism and gender roles is made less clear — Don argues that it is part of the conditioning capitalism requires if it is to continue.

The economic system is such a force dominating people's lives that no real liberation is possible without first overthrowing the capitalist system. Thus Don argues that we should direct our demands for an end to discrimination not at the ruling class and state government, but rather at the organised Labour movement which is the only group with the potential power to overthrow the state and end economic exploitation.

Attempts at communal living and 'lifestyle' politics are good because they show us what will be possible in the future, but this kind of politics can only have a limited effect since it does not challenge the economic system on an organised mass basis. Gay people do not form a united economically oppressed group, neither do we have a geographical unity around which we organise. Only the working class has this power.

The above is too short to do justice to Don's argument, but I hope it summarises fairly his main political arguments. I would now like to add my own comments.

The weakest point in the argument seems to be the lack of a clear connection between male supremacy and capitalism. I think that Don is so fixated on the economic evils of capitalism that he assumes that everything else must be part of a very elaborate confidence trick arranged to keep the system under control. But what is obviously true is that male supremacy existed long before capitalism, and so the domination of women cannot be said to be specifically caused by capitalism. I would argue the other way round — that capitalism is male domination developed to its highest form, where the male values of domination, aggression, competition, individualism, inhumanity and exploitation are imposed on all aspects of life. Male supremacy is not an outgrowth of capitalism, rather capitalism is the highest form of masculine supremacy.

Seeing things this way round has political consequences. I would argue that men and workers will be incapable of authentic collective action (with women and children) until they take notice of the demands of women's and gay liberation and change themselves, and *stop* oppressing gays, women and children. They will be incapable of taking over the factories and organising things collectively until they take our demands seriously.

In this I think communal living and lifestyle politics have a large part to play. Living together has been the only way I've known that gay men have really been able to get to grips with the way we've been messed about by straight society, the only way we can begin to understand what we really want. Only when we discover what we really want, can we then find ways of getting it.

In the long term Don may be right that communes and such like only have a limited role to play in an overall change, but at this time and for us I think they are very important. Part of communal living has been not-working (unemployed and sharing whatever money we can come by while not-working). We probably won't be able to do this for the rest of our lives, but I think it is an important thing to do for a while. The most common question we are asked (by workers) is, 'How do you fill up your time?' People seem *afraid* of not-working, of not being told what to do, for most of their lives, dreading retirement when they'll have times on their hands and 'nothing to do'. Until people lose the fear of taking control of their lives, we're not going to be revolutionary.

Rumour has it that Don is in danger of being thrown out of IS for his trouble in raising these issues. These are things we should talk about more.

Bob Mellors

Welcome to Scotland

First of all, gay people in Scotland are no different in themselves than anywhere else. We have the same miseries, personal crises, joys, despairs and happiness as gay people anywhere else. That's personally. So what makes Scotland so different? Why the fuss? If the gays are no different, then what is? The situation they live in. Scotland's history, its temperament, its pattern of economic and cultural behaviour, have brought about a fairly unique national atmosphere. The main event that has moulded this atmosphere has been the Reformation. This country still pervades of staunch Calvinistic thought — even the atheists in Scotland seem like 'presbyterian atheists'.

I think I should explain this a little further (or try to). Every person who has grown up in Scotland will have quite a bit of Calvinism instilled in his/her very nature; even if she/he has been brought up in a broadminded, independent family situation that person will still somehow accumulate some attitudes which can be directly attributed to the advent of Scottish Calvinism (or Knoxism). I am a homosexual, I call myself a Marxist, wear freaky clothes and do all the naughty deviant things a Dirty Pinko Commie Pervert Hippy can be expected to do, but I *still* see, from time to time, some outrageously reactionary Calvinist attitudes seeping out (especially in relation to things like 'love', 'fidelity', monogamy, etc.). Naturally these particular attitudes offend me intellectually but nevertheless I must recognise that they exist in me, ruthlessly conditioned into me since birth by the very atmosphere of this country. I like to think I am attempting to rid myself of these attitudes, but it's a pretty arduous task getting rid of 20 years of pollutive teachings and educational diarrhoea.

I feel I must stress how difficult it is to *really* rebel in Scotland. Oh yes, it's easy enough growing your hair long and putting on some ratty clothes and a button badge, smoking dope and saying 'man' at the end of every sentence, but it doesn't take much perception to see through that 'revolution', does it? I am quite sure we all know countless people whose 'revolution' doesn't go beyond just plain naughtiness. These people are just Mum and Dad with long hair. And I'm also sure most of us know how fucking difficult it is to get a much deeper and more thorough revolution going on inside our own heads, never mind anyone else's. Well, that task in a Scottish setting seems to take on multiple proportions. In Scotland, the Feu Duties are still payable when buying a house (these are duties to the Church of Scotland), the pubs close on the stroke of 10 p.m. and you can't even get a drink in the afternoon or on a Sunday (except in some hotels), all-male pubs are still commonplace, etc. etc. etc.

Or maybe this will give you a better picture. At a recently held teach-in on homosexuality in Edinburgh, which was organised for the most part by gay people, there were *four* clergymen on the platform and a large contingent of clerical collars in the audience. (GLF was not represented *at all* on the platform.) You might say, as we did at first, that is fucking ridiculous — but it's not. If you had lived here you'd realise just how reasonable it is that so many clergy should be present at a homosexuality teach-in, simply because of the amount of influence they and their Moral Welfare Committees wield in the formation of attitudes in this country.

In Scotland, the men are very much Men, and the women — well they know their place, and ne'er the twain shall meet (except in Church-condoned procreative acts, that is!). Working-class kids who have been constantly told that they are educational and occupational failures try desperately to succeed in the only way left — through their masculinity. Gangs form and fight, etc. and it'd be stupid of me to try and deny the fact that there's a hell of a lot of violence in Scotland — and all because of the rancid system which is oppressing their class. But most important of all, through all crises, these kids must hang on to their manliness (it's all they have left that can gain *them* some 'respect' for a change; aggression, arrogance, ruthlessness, toughness, strength, 'bravery', etc. — all these, plus a big helping of pig-headedness, add up to Manliness), because if they fail in that then they will be considered all-round failures and society sees no justification in their existence (except, perhaps, as society's scapegoat).

However, a more sophisticated version of the big sex-identity bit seems to be the be-all and end-all of existence in middle-class homes. The Scottish middle-class seem to know, in their heart of heart (perhaps through some Divine Inspiration) that Darwinism *is* a heresy, that Adam and Eve really did exist and that they provide a fine example to 20th century life! Max Weber paralleled the Protestant Ethic with the Spirit of Capitalism and I can think of few other places where the relationship is more evident than in Scotland.

As I say, this country owes most of its most profound heritage to Knox and Calvin, and the sexual attitudes of the Scottish power elite is the area where ultra-conservative, puritanical reaction gives its most undying concentration. I suppose most of you will have heard of the late Councillor John Kidd's opinions on how he thought it desirable that the police should set dogs on all those queers that are trying to turn Edinburgh into the 'London of the North'. And at the teach-in on homosexuality we were all horrified to hear the amazing tirade of fascist rhetoric spilling forth from the mouth of the Reverend John Grey. Things like how homosexuality is a misfortune and how he feels sorry that we won't experience the joys of having and raising a family, and how he hopes the Church will continue to support the treatment of homosexuals! Sick and dangerous stuff perhaps, but the sickest thing about it is that there are many more millions like them — most of whom aren't either rich, powerful, or reverend! It's when you realise this that you begin to feel and see what you are up against.

Just by our very existence we are an offence and a threat to this system. However, it seems to us that the Scottish Cerberus has many more heads than the English/Welsh ones. Often we feel just like submitting, joining with SMG, working on the law reform bill along with all those remarkable QCs, peers, councillors, professors etc., but submission seems much more difficult than just carrying on. We don't do much except talk and hold discos, but I'm sure everybody knows the feeling when you realise and value the fact that there are more than one of you, even if it is only two, or three, or four — that's something. But I'm also sure we know the intense frustration of just talking, especially when your words don't seem to get any further than those other persons' ear-lobes (assuming that they even get that far).

My comments on SMG and law reform may be taken wrongly. I have little doubt as to the service SMG has provided to the gay population in Scotland and its contribution to the position regarding homosexuality. I also have a certain amount of admiration for those involved in the drafting of the law reform bill, but not all of us are prepared to stop there. Not all of us are content to settle for ages of consent, gay churches and marriages etc. Some of us, thank fuck, see more to being gay (and more to life, for that matter) than a wedding-band on your left hand, even if it was put there by a member of your own sex.

I think that our challenge in Scotland is quite different than that in the rest of the country — our still waters seem to run more stagnant, more putrid and deeper than the rest of Britain's. I can only blame history for this. Perhaps I am being unfair in claiming this and by pushing our uniqueness so much — maybe I feel a little 'sour grapes' because of the lack of support and solidarity (perhaps this was through lack of understanding) which the Gay Liberation movement in Scotland, and I would imagine, Northern Ireland, has received from the English movement. I am not claiming that the struggle in the rest of the country is less worthy and small in comparison to ours, only that it is completely different and does not put the same pressures and demands upon those involved, as the struggle in Scotland does on us.

It isn't just difficult in Scotland to come out as being gay, it's fucking hard to be yourself, whether you're gay or not, when you are faced with reaction in every public and national sector and worse, when your own pocket-size, personal, made-to-measure Calvinism (remember? the one we inherit from Mum and Dad?) starts rearing its ugly head.

However, to know the Scottish climate and temperament and why the Scots are as they are, you would really need to live in the exhilarating and stultifying atmosphere of Scotland. (The Scottish Tourist Board will love me for that.)

Everyone knows how fond we are of quoting Burns (ha, fucking ha!). Well here are two:

In politics, if thou would'st mix, and mean thy fortunes be, bear this in mind, be deaf and blind — *let rich folks hear and see.*

— and a few words of wisdom —

There's none that's blest of human-kind, but the cheerful and the *gay.*

Martin (Edinburgh GLF)

Gay Women Together

> 'Following custom, the term "homosexual" refers to male homosexual here . . . Whatever its potentiality in sexual politics, female homosexuality is currently so dead an issue that when male homosexuality gains a grudging tolerance, in women the event is observed in scorn or in silence.'
>
> footnote, Kate Millett's *Sexual Politics*.

We all know why women, traditionally, have no concept of their own exploitation, infrequently join any organisation, if they're gay or bisexual become aware of this later than gay men, find it harder to hear about gay meeting-places, join gay organisations less frequently than gay men. We also know that once they meet each other — usually in meetings when we're outnumbered by gay men — it's still difficult to relate to each other, to be loving, to stay together, without feeling guilty about it, without feeling that men ought to be included. We have several thousand years' backlog of communication to catch up on, and not even the sense of community that a lot of groups of gay men have, because we don't very often meet together as any sort of group (unless it's in a pub or a club).

To the extent that a homophile community exists in Britain at the moment, it exists because of the cross-fertilisation of ideas produced by Women's Lib and GLF in the States and the existence and activity of GLF in this country. For the first time ever we have the beginnings of a community that we belong to, that's held together by love and caring for each other, that doesn't just depend on sexual preference and sexual activity, and that has a political consciousness. And this is happening in a lot of CHE groups as well as GLF ones.

Where are gay women in all this? Mostly, outside of London, as very small groups and individuals inside male-oriented and dominated groups in large towns and cities.

Most gay and bisexual women don't hear about GLF or CHE, or if they do are frightened off because they think they're 'men's groups'. And if we're honest about it, up till now neither of them has made a real consistent effort to get more women to join them. And why should they anyway? Women should be doing it.

As *gay* women we need to do two main things. We need to develop our position within the theory of sexual politics (let's find where we're at, baby!) and use this as a basis for action. It ought to be relatively easy — everything that's been done so far has been done by women and is mainly about women. Women like Kate Millett and Shulamith Firestone are saying that 'patriarchy' is a system of power that exists in all societies and at all times (to date), and that it exists independently of any type of economic system (although it obviously operates through economic systems); and this is a definite move towards producing a feminist, and not a socialist, analysis of power and politics. And it's on this that the rest of their analysis of the position of women is built. And it's from this that gay lib ideology originates. We also need to 'organise' (no, I don't mean bureaucratic structures, minute-taking and all the rest of it) and to communicate with each other (let's put our feet where our head's at, baby!). We need to be able to meet and talk to each other and to use every means we can to get publicity, so that all the thousands of gay women who don't hear about any gay groups hear about us.

Manchester's a comparatively good place to live in. It has quite a few gay clubs and pubs; and three gay groups, one of which has existed for two and a half years. But until the women's group started last November, the total number of women who came to any of these groups' meetings was only about thirty, and only about fifteen or twenty stayed in contact with them (apart from parties and discos). About forty women came to the first women's meeting — and most of us had never seen so many gay women together in one room that wasn't a club; although meetings only average about twenty, about sixty women are in contact with the group and at least two or three get in contact every week. We've had a half-hour spot on local radio, ads in the local paper, posters (with a telephone number) in gay pubs and clubs, colleges and universities, lavatories, libraries and shops. We meet every fortnight and talk (about just about everything), we have parties and discos, we go out together; and we're friends with each other.

Obviously it's not perfect, no one's trying to pretend that it is; but it's a beginning — and we need more beginners.

Liz Stanley